To
Rev. W. T. Sproll. D. D
with the kind regards
of the Compiler
Mrs J. Hamilton

July 29/64

Drifted Snow-Flakes;

OR,

POETICAL GATHERINGS

FROM

Many Authors

FOR SALE AT THE
PROTESTANT EPISCOPAL BOOK SOCIETY,
1224 CHESTNUT STREET,
PHILADELPHIA.

J. FAGAN & SON, STEREOTYPERS, PHILADELPHIA.

Introduction.

A FEW of the poems contained in this volume have already appeared in print as "Gleanings for Letters;" others of them have been selected by friends, and sent to me for the same purpose. But many of them have not been published before; being the effusions of earnest and devout minds, speaking aloud the sentiments breathed in the sick chamber; or, when the heart was crushed with sorrow, joyful through hope, or jubilant with praise. I found my collection had become quite a *little heap*,—wafted hither by the breath of friendship, or the desire to do good. And it occurred to me that I could not do better than to spread it out in a book; hoping that some hearts might be cheered, comforted, and refreshed by its contents, as they journeyed heavenward.

J. H.

April, 1864.

CONTENTS.

Drifted Snow-Flakes.

The Cross.

"Take my yoke upon you, and learn of me . . . . my yoke is easy, and my burden is light."—*Matt.* xi. 20, 30.

MY heart was full of happiness,
  Each scene around me bright,
I leaned on the "Beloved One,"
  His candle gave me light;
I thought such joy would still be mine,
  Such bliss would never cease,
And gladly published all around
  That wisdom's paths are peace.

But soon a cloud obscured my path,
  A *cross* before me lay;
I knew it was for me to bear,
  And yet I turned away;

The voice of my Beloved spake,
  Yet stern it seemed to be,
He pointed to the cross, and said,
  "Take it and follow me."

Father! Oh! Father! ask not *this*,
  'Tis more than I can bear,
Lay any other burden on,
  But *this* in mercy spare;
Let me move but one step aside,
  And so escape this loss;
Father! thy feeble child will sink
  Beneath this weary cross.

My prayer unheard, unheeded sped,
  Or was—if heard—denied;
He hedged my way so closely in,
  I could not turn aside;
Yet still I strove to break the fence,
  Rebelled against the rod,
And struggled sorely 'gainst Thy will,
  My Saviour and my God.

But He who loved me at the first,
  Still loved me to the end,
And spite of all my waywardness,
  Remained my faithful Friend;

He bore with all my hard complaints,
'Gainst my rebellion strove,
And showed me that this dreaded cross
Was sent in *perfect love.*

I stopped, I raised it up—and lo!
The heavy weight was gone;
My Saviour bore the load for me,
I was not left *alone.*
Then grateful, humbled in the dust,
Once more my path I trod,
Feeling how *light* the burden is
Which we can cast on God.

The Gathering Home.

THEY are gathering homeward from every land
One by one,
As their weary feet touch the shining strand
One by one,
Their brows are enclosed in a golden crown,
Their travel-stained garments are all laid down,
And, clothed in white raiment, they rest on the mead,
Where the Lamb loveth his chosen to lead,
One by one.

Before they rest they pass through the strife
One by one,
Through the waters of death they enter life
One by one;
To some are the floods of the river still,
As they ford on their way to the heavenly hill;
To others the waves run fiercely and wild,
Yet they reach the home of the undefiled,
One by one.

We, too, shall come to the river side
One by one,
We are nearer its waters each eventide
One by one.
We can hear the noise and dash of the stream
Now and again through our life's deep dream;
Sometimes the floods all the banks o'erflow,
Sometimes in ripples and small waves go,
One by one.

Jesus! Redeemer! we look to Thee,
One by one;
We lift up our voices tremblingly
One by one;
The waves of the river are dark and cold,
We know not the spots where our feet may hold;
Thou, who didst pass through in deep midnight,
Strengthen us—send us the staff and the light,
One by one.

Plant Thou thy feet beside as we tread,
One by one;
On Thee let us lean each drooping head,
One by one;
Let but Thy strong arm around us be twined,
We shall cast all our fears and cares to the wind.
Saviour! Redeemer! with Thee full in view,
Smilingly, gladsomely, shall we pass through,
One by one.

MARY E. LESLIE.

The Day Laborer.

"In the morning sow thy seed, and in the evening withhold not thine hand: for thou knowest not whether shall prosper, either this or that, or whether they shall both be alike good."—*Eccles.* xi. 6.

SOW ye beside all waters,
Where the dew of heaven may fall;
Ye shall reap if ye be not weary,
For the Spirit breathes o'er all.
Sow, though the thorns may wound thee—
One wore the thorns for thee;
And though the cold world scorn thee,
Patient and hopeful be.

Sow ye beside all waters,
With a blessing and a prayer:
Name Him whose hand upholds us,
And sow thou everywhere.

Sow, though the rock repel thee,
In its cold and sterile pride;
Some cleft there may be riven,
Where the little seed may hide.
Fear not, for some will flourish;
And, though the tares abound,
Like the willows by the waters
Will the scattered grain be found.
Work while the daylight lasteth,
Ere the shades of night come on;
Ere the Lord of the vineyard cometh,
And the laborer's work is done.

Work! in the wild waste places,
Though none thy love may own;
God guides the down of the thistle
The wand'ring wind hath sown.
Will Jesus chide thy weakness,
Or call thy labor vain?
The word that for Him thou barest,
Shall return to him again.
On!—with thine heart in heaven,
Thy strength—in thy Master's might,
Till the wild waste places blossom
In the warmth of a Saviour's light.

Watch not the clouds above thee
  Let the whirlwind round thee sweep;
God may the seed-time give thee,
  But another's hand may reap.
Have faith, though ne'er beholding
  The seed burst from its tomb,
Thou know'st not which may perish,
  Or what be spared to bloom.
Room on the narrowest ridges
  The ripen'd grain will find,
That the Lord of the harvest coming
  In the harvest sheaves may bind.

What Then?

AFTER the joys of earth,
  After its songs of mirth,
After its hours of light,
After its dreams so bright—
          What then?

Only an empty name,
Only a weary frame,
Only a conscious smart,
Only an aching heart.

After this empty name,
After this weary frame,
After this conscious smart,
After this aching heart—
What then?

Only a sad farewell
To a world loved too well,
Only a silent bed
With the forgotten dead.

After this sad farewell
To a world loved too well,
After this silent bed
With the forgotten dead—
What then?

Oh! then—the Judgment throne!
Oh! then—the last hope—gone!
Then, all the woes that dwell
In an eternal HELL!

What Then?

AFTER the Christian's tears,
After his fights and fears,
After his weary cross,
"All things below but loss"—
What then?

Oh! then—a holy calm,
Resting on JESUS' arm,
Oh! then—a deeper love
For the pure Home above.

After this holy calm,
This rest on JESUS' arm,
After this deepen'd love
For the pure Home above—
What then?

Oh! then—work for Him,
Perishing souls to win,
Then JESUS' presence near,
Death's darkest hour to cheer.

And when the work is done,
When the last soul is won,
When JESUS' love and power
Have cheered the dying hour—
What then?

Oh! then—the Crown is given!
Oh! then—the rest in Heaven!
Endless life, in endless day,
Sin and sorrow pass'd away.

E. J.

To One Departed.

ARE we remembered in the world above us?
Do fond eyes watch us from the distant sky?
Or fades our image from the hearts that loved us?
Answer me!—answer to my bitter cry!

Come to me, loved one! I am sad and lonely,
Though friends to cheer me, gather round the while;
'Twas in thy heart that mine was mirrored only,
And I am pining for thy voice and smile.

I know that I am earthly—thou immortal—
Still in the flesh am I—thou, glorified;
Yet, is there no return through Heaven's bright portal?
Cannot my love recall thee to my side?

Only one hour! I would not seek to stay thee,
Nor ask that thou should'st linger here below;
I would but see the glories that array thee,
And hear once more thy accents, soft and low.

I will not shrink—I wait thee—none are near me—
Think not I fear the splendor that is thine!
An *unknown* spirit I might dread—but fear *thee*?
Stronger than terror is a love like mine.

My friend! my friend! oh! *is* there no returning
For those who reach, as victors, life's blest goal?
Or is it that my spirit's passionate yearning
Can now awake no echo in thy soul?

Alas! 'tis vain! the human heart that loved me
Lies stilled and pulseless in death's dreamless rest;
And the soul, far, far,—e'en on earth—above me,
Will stoop no more my lonely path to bless.

Yet, yet,—oh! *must* I deem myself forsaken?
Nay, but I will believe thee near me yet;
Oh! all the brightness from my life were taken,
Were I indeed to think thou could'st forget.

I will believe that, though unseen and voiceless,
Thy blessed presence is about me still;
That thou over every step of mine rejoicest,
That leads me onward to the heavenly hill.

My spirit-love! my seraph-guardian! ever
Hover around my dark and lonely way;
Though the thick veil of flesh and sense may sever
My soul from thine for many a weary day.

If thou mayst never bend in brightness o'er me
While in its house of clay my spirit dwells,
Help me to tread the path that lies before me,
And reach the world where there are no farewells.

R. A. R.

Assurance in Christ.

The First Epistle of John, v. 1–13.

CAN it be right for me to go
  On in this dark, uncertain way;
Say "I believe," and yet not know
  Whether my sins are put away?

Not know my trespasses forgiven
  Until I meet Him in the air,
Not know that I shall get to Heaven
  Until I wake and find me there.

Not know my state, 'till on my brow
  Beams the celestial diadem:
Why surely all the world will know
  That I'm a pardoned sinner then.

Must clouds and darkness vail my brow
  Until I dwell with saints in light?
And must I walk in darkness now
  Because I cannot walk by sight?

And shall I just begin to say
  "Father, thine every word is true,"
And cast my doubts and fears away
  When all the world will own it too?

Is this the way to treat the God
  Who bids me love and trust him now?
Is this the way to use the Word,
  Given to guide me here below?

How can I forth to sinners go,
  And tell of grace so rich and free,
If all the while I do not know
  Whether that grace has smiled on me?

How can it be my joy to dwell
  On the rich power of Jesus' blood,
If all the while I cannot tell
  That it HAS sealed MY peace with God?

How can I be like Christ below—
  How like my Lord in witness shine—
Unless with conscious joy I know
  HIS Father and HIS God as MINE?

O crush this cruel unbelief,
  These needless, shameful doubts remove;
And suffer me no more to grieve
  The God whom I do really love.

Father, I would, and O how blest
  Whilst thus I supplicate to know
That ONE, of all Thy mind possessed,
  Thy Spirit supplicateth too

I would, with humble gladness, say,
  I rest on what my Lord hath done;
And evermore on earth display
  The lovely image of Thy Son.

I would, whate'er the world might say,
  Whate'er by flesh might be endured,
Be more and more each passing day
  Made like unto my gracious Lord.

Sweet posture THUS on earth to stay,
  And not be taken by surprise;
But catch the earliest dawn of day,
  And see the "Morning Star arise!"

Blessed is the Man whom Thou Chasteneth.

The following beautiful lines are by Sir Robert Grant, late Governor-General of India.

O SAVIOUR! whose mercy, severe in its kindness,
  Has chastened my wanderings and guided my way,
Ador'd be the power which illumined my blindness,
  And weaned me from phantoms that smiled to betray.

Enchanted with all that was dazzling and fair,
I followed the rainbow—I caught at the toy;
And still in displeasures Thy goodness was there,
Disappointing the hope and defeating the joy.

The blossom blushed bright — but a worm was below;
The moonlight shone fair—there was blight in the beam;
Sweet whispered the breeze—but it whispered of woe,
And bitterness flowed in the soft-flowing stream.

So, cured of my folly,—yet cured but in part,—
I turned to the refuge Thy pity displayed;
And still did this eager and credulous heart
Weave visions of promise that bloomed but to fade.

I thought that the course of the pilgrim to heaven
Would be bright as the summer, and glad as the morn;
Thou show'dst me the path — it was dark and uneven—
All rugged with rock, and all tangled with thorn.

I dreamed of celestial reward and renown;
I grasped at the triumph which blesses the brave—
I asked for the palm-branch, the robe, and the crown;
I asked—and Thou show'dst me a cross and a grave.

Subdued and instructed, at length, to Thy will,
My hopes and my longings I fain would resign;
O give me the heart that can wait and be still,
Nor know of a wish nor a pleasure but Thine.

There *are* mansions exempted from sin and from woe;
But they stand in a region by mortals untrod;
There are rivers of joy—but they roll not below;
There is rest—but it dwells in the presence of God.

Only Waiting.

ONLY waiting till the shadows
Are a little longer grown;
Only waiting till the glimmer
Of the day's last beam is flown;

Till the night of earth is faded
  From the heart, once full of day;
Till the stars of heaven are breaking
  Through the twilight soft and gray.

Only waiting till the reapers
  Have the last sheaf gathered home;
For the summer time is faded,
  And the autumn winds have come.
Quickly! reapers, gather quickly
  The last ripe hours of my heart;
For the bloom of life is withered,
  And I hasten to depart.

Only waiting till the angels
  Open wide the mystic gate,
At whose feet I long have lingered
  Weary, poor, and desolate.
Even now I hear their footsteps,
  And their voices far away;
If they call me, I am waiting,
  Only waiting to obey.

Only waiting till the shadows
  Are a little longer grown;
Only waiting till the glimmer
  Of the day's last beam is flown.
Then from out the gathering darkness,
  Holy, deathless stars shall rise,
By whose light my soul shall gladly
  Tread its pathway to the skies.

"Behold, the Bridegroom Cometh!"

BEHOLD, a Royal Bridegroom
  Hath called me for His bride!
I joyfully make ready*
  And hasten to His side.
He is a Royal Bridegroom,
  But I am very poor!
Of low estate He chose me
  To show His love the more:
For He hath purchased for me
  Such goodly rich array,—
Oh, surely never Bridegroom
  Gave gifts like His away.

When first upon the mountains,
  I, in the vale below,
Beheld Him waiting for me,
  Heard His command to go,
I, poorest in the valley,
  Oh, how could I prepare
To meet His royal presence?
  How could I make me fair?
Ah! in His love He sent me
  A garment clean and white:†

* Rev. xix. 7. † Rev. xix. 8.

And promised broidered raiment
  All glorious in His sight.
And then He gave me glimpses
  Of the jewels for my hair,*
And the ornament most precious†
  For His chosen bride to wear.

First in my tears I washed me,—
  They could not make me clean:
A fountain then He showed me,‡
  Strange until then unseen!
So close I'd lived beside it
  For many weary years,
Yet passing by the fountain,
  Had bathed me in my tears.
Oh, love, oh, grace, that showed it!§
  Revealed its cleansing power!
How could I choose but hasten
  To meet Him from that hour.

I said, delay no longer!
  He surely will provide
All for the toilsome journey,
  Up the steep mountain side.
He sought me in the valley—
  He knows my utmost need;

* 2 Tim. iv. 8. † 1 Pet. iii. 4.
‡ Zech. xiii. 1. § Rom. iii. 4.

But He's a Royal Bridegroom,
  I shall be rich indeed.
Rich in His pardoning mercies,—
  Bounties that never cease:
Rich in His loving kindness,
  Rich in His joy and peace.
So then I took the Raiment,
  And the jewels that He sent;
And, gazing on His beauty,
  I up the hillside went.

And still with feeble footsteps,
  And turning oft astray,
I go to meet the Bridegroom,
  Though stumbling by the way
I soil my royal garments
  With earth whene'er I fall;
I break and mar my ornaments,
  But He will know them all.
For it was He who gave them;
  Will He forget His own?
Ah! for the love He bore me,
  He called! will He disown?

He sent His Guide to guide me:
  He knew how blind, how frail
The children of the valley:—
  He knew my love would fail.

He knew the mists above me
  Would hide Him from my sight,
And I, in darkness groping,
  Would wander from the right.
I know that I must follow
  Slow when I fain would soar:
That step by step thus upward,
  My Guide must go before.

Cleave close, dear Guide, and lead me!
  I cannot go aright!
Through all that doth beset me,
  Keep, keep me close in sight!
'Tis but a little longer;
  Methinks the end I see:
Oh! matchless love and mercy,
  The Bridegroom waits for me;
Waits, to present me faultless,
  Before His Father's throne;
His comeliness my beauty, *
  His righteousness my own.

* Phil. iii. 21.

Submission.

"The cup that my Father hath given me, shall I not drink it."

MUSING on all my Father's love, (how sweet it is,)
Methought I heard a gentle voice—
"Child, here's a cup;
I've mixed it; drink it up."
My heart did sink, I could no more rejoice.

"Father, dost thou not love thy child? Then why this cup?"
"One day, my child, I said to thee—
'Here is a flower,
Plucked from a beauteous bower;'
Didst thou complain, or take it thankfully?

"One day I gave thee pleasant fruit from a choice tree;
How pleased, how grateful thou didst seem;
Thou saidst, 'I love
Thee, faithful may I prove;'
Thy heart was full, with joy thine eyes did beam

"That flower was mine, that fruit was mine, this
cup is mine;
And all that's in it comes from me."
"Father, I'm still;
Forgive my naughty will,
But what's in the cup; may I look in and see?"

"Thou see! my child, thou must not see! Christ
only saw
His destined cup of bitter gall.
Only believe;
Meekly the cup receive;
And know that love and wisdom mixed it all."

"O, Father, must it be?" "It must, my child!"
"Then give
The needed medicine.
Be by my side;
Only thy face don't hide;
I'll drink it all; it must be good; 'tis thine!"

Fleeing to God.

UNDER the shadow of Thy wings, my Father,
'Till these calamities be overpast!
In that sure refuge let my spirit gather
Strength to look calmly back upon the past.

Be merciful to me! for thoughts that crush me
Lie like an incubus upon my breast;
Only Thy voice, Omnipotent, can hush me
Into the quiet e'en of seeming rest.

Thou knowest—Thou only—the dark chain that binds me,
The heavy chain which eats into my soul;
The links of adamant which have entwined me,
Binding each feeling in their chill control.

Oh! what is life but one long, long endurance
Of this dull, heavy weight on heart and brain?
Speak to my spirit—speak the strong assurance
That nothing Thou ordainest is in vain.

Trembling amid the turmoils of existence,
Oh! let me grasp a more than mortal arm;
Father! my Father! be not at a distance
When earth's dark phantoms Thy weak child alarm.

Under Thy shadow! Fear cannot appal me
If in the Rock of Ages surely hid;
Under Thy shadow! Harm cannot befall me
If Thou,—All-wise! All-merciful! forbid.

Nearer to Thee!—my Saviour! my Redeemer!
In earth, or heaven, whom hath my soul but Thee?
Though for an instant, as some feverish dreamer
Grasps at the treasures which he seems to see.

I, too, have dreamed, and waked to find "illusion"
Inscribed on all I sought to make my own;
And turning from my idols in confusion,
I dedicate my life to Thee alone.

Under the shadow of Thy wing abiding,
Close to a sympathizing Saviour's side,
In the sure promise of His love confiding,
Why should I shrink, though earthly ills betide?

Oh! if the soul grew strong through suffering only,
If but through trial it may reach its goal,
I will rejoice, although my way be lonely,
And all Thy waves and billows o'er me roll.

Yes! I will praise Thee! though my tears are falling
Upon the trembling harp-string as I sing;
Am I not safe — though grief my soul is thralling—
Under the shadow of my Father's wing?

R. A. R.

MOUNT HOLLY, February 5th, 1853.

The Cruse that Faileth Not.

"It is more blessed to give than to receive."

IS thy cruse of comfort wasting? rise and share it with another,
And through all the years of famine, it shall serve thee and thy brother;
Love divine will fill thy storehouse, or thy handful still renew;
Scanty fare for one, will often make a royal feast for two.

For the heart grows rich in giving; all its wealth is living grain;
Seeds, which mildew in the garner, scattered, fill with gold the plain.
Is thy burden hard and heavy? Do thy steps drag wearily?
Help to bear thy brother's burden; God will bear both it and thee.

Numb and weary on the mountains, wouldst thou sleep amidst thee snow?
Chafe that frozen form beside thee, and together both shall glow.
Art thou stricken in life's battle; many wounded round thee moan;
Lavish on their wounds thy balsams, and that balm shall heal thine own.

Is the heart a well left empty? None but God
its void can fill;
Nothing but a ceaseless fountain can its ceaseless
longing still.
Is the heart a living power? Self-entwined, its
strength sinks low;
It can only live in loving, and by serving love
will grow.

Though I be Nothing.

MY Father! can I learn so hard a task?
Thou must; no more, my child, of you I
ask
Than He hath done,
My well beloved Son.
Must I be nothing? Must I nothing do?
Nothing, my child; Christ hath done all for you.
You cannot buy,
The price is all too high;
Freely I give,
Only believe and live.
Enough! give Thou the humble heart, and I
consent;
Oh! make me nothing and therewith content.

My gain is loss,
My trust is in the Cross;
Hold me, I'm weak, I fall;
Be Thou mine all.
And give me, Lord, in all, some quiet place,
Where I can work, and yet behold Thy face,
While Thou shalt bid me say,
"Keep my feet steadfast in the way;
They must not tire,
Till Thou bid me
Come up higher."
E'en then above, let me be nothing still,
That Christ alone the Heaven of heavens may fill.
Yet set me, Lord,
A little glowing Gem
Upon His Diadem,
To shed my tiny ray
Among the splendors of His crowning day;
Though unperceived, I should like to shine,
A tribute glory on that brow divine;
And let me raise
One little note of praise,
Though scarcely heard among the myriad voices,
When the redeemed Church in Christ rejoices;
So may it blend
With angel hallelujahs, which ascend,
A lowly offering to my Saviour friend.
Lord, I am nothing, Christ in all must shine;
Do with me as Thou wilt, for *I am Thine.*

The Changed Cross.

IT was a time of sadness, and my heart—
Although it knew and felt the better part—
Felt wearied with the conflict and the strife,
And all the needful discipline of life.

And while I thought on these as given to me—
My trial tests of faith and love to be—
It seemed as if I never could be sure
That faithful to the end I should endure.

And thus no longer trusting to His might,
Who says, "we walk by faith, and not by sight,"
Doubting, and almost yielding to despair,
The thought arose—my cross I cannot bear.

For heavier its weight must surely be
Than those of others which I daily see;
Oh! if I might another burden choose,
Methinks I should not fear my crown to lose.

A solemn silence reigned on all around—
E'en Nature's voices uttered not a sound;
The evening shadows seemed of peace to tell,
And sleep upon my weary spirit fell.

A moment's pause, and then a heavenly light
Beamed full upon my wondering, raptured sight;
Angels on silvery wings seemed everywhere,
And angels' music thrilled the balmy air.

Then One, more fair than all the rest to see—
One to whom all the others bowed the knee—
Came gently to me, as I trembling lay,
And, "Follow me," He said, "I am the way."

Then speaking thus, He led me far above:
And there, beneath a canopy of love,
Crosses of divers shape and size were seen,
Larger and smaller than my own had been.

And one there was most beauteous to behold—
A little one, with jewels set in gold:
Ah! this, methought, I can with comfort wear,
For it will be an easy one to bear.

And so the little cross I quickly took,
But all at once my frame beneath it shook;
The sparkling jewels fair were they to *see*,
But far too heavy was their *weight* for me.

This may not be, I cried, and looked again,
To see if there was any here could ease my pain;
But one by one I passed them slowly by,
Till on a lovely one I cast my eye.

Fair flowers around its sculptured form entwined,
And grace and beauty seemed in it combined;
Wondering, I gazed, and still I wondered more,
To think so many should have passed it o'er.

But, oh! that form so beautiful to see
Soon made its hidden sorrows known to me;
Thorns lay beneath those flowers and colors fair:
Sorrowing, I said, "This cross I may not bear."

And so it was with each and all around—
No one to suit my *need* could there be found;
Weeping, I laid each heavy burden down,
As my Guide gently said, "No cross, no crown!"

At length to Him I raised my saddened heart;
He knew its sorrows, bid its doubts depart;
"Be not afraid," He said, "but trust in me—
My perfect love shall now be shown to thee."

And then, with lightened eyes and willing feet,
Again I turned, my earthly cross to meet,
With forward footsteps, turning not aside,
For fear some sudden evil might betide.

And there, in the prepared, appointed way—
Listening to hear, and ready to obey—
A cross I quickly found of plainest form,
With only words of love inscribed thereon.

With thankfulness I raised it from the rest,
And joyfully acknowledged it the best—
The only one of all the many there
That I could feel was good for me to bear.

And while I thus my chosen one confessed,
I saw a heavenly brightness on it rest;
And as I bent, my burden to sustain,
I recognized my own old cross again!

But oh! how different did it seem to be
Now I had learned its preciousness to see!
No longer could I unbelieving say,
Perhaps another is a better way.

Ah, no! henceforth my own desire shall be,
That He who knows me best shall choose for me;
And so whate'er His love sees good to send,
I'll trust it's best, because He knows the end.

"For my thoughts are not your thoughts, saith the Lord," —*Isaiah*, l. 8.

"For I know the thoughts that I think towards you—thoughts of peace, and not of evil, to give you an expected end."—*Jer*. xxix. 11.

And when that happy time shall come, of endless peace and rest,
We shall look back upon our path and say—It was the best.

"Is it Well?"

TRAVELER through these scenes of sorrow,
Weary with the march of life;
Hoping nothing for the morrow
But renewed and ceaseless strife:
In thy sky no ray of gladness
Of a brighter day to tell,
Overwhelmed with grief and sadness,
Weary traveller, "Is it well?"

Storm and tempest howl around thee,
Clouds obscure thy toilsome way;
Gloom, and night, and fear, surround thee
Yet for light thou may'st not stay;
Onward, 'mid the darkness groping,
Struggling through life's deepest dell,
Scarce to reach its outlet hoping;—
Trembling pilgrim, "Is it well?"

All that thou had'st craved possessing,
Hast been wrested from thy grasp;
And beneath each fancied blessing
Thou hast found an hidden asp:

Disappointed, worn, and weary,
  Crushed with woes thou may'st not tell;
Earth and all its prospects dreary,
  Tell me, sad one, "Is it well?"

"Is it well" that God has taken
  All that thou had'st deemed thine own?
"Is it well" that grief has shaken
  Hope forever from her throne?
Death has of thy friends bereft thee,
  Borne them to the grave's dark cell;
Not an earthly joy is left thee,—
  Answer Christian, "is it well?"

Can'st thou still with meek submission
  Kiss the hand that wields the rod?
See'st thou with faith's trusting vision,
  Love in all that comes from God?
Is there rest for thee in heaven?
  Hop'st thou there with Christ to dwell?
Ah! howe'er by tempests driven,
  Then, believer, "It is well?"

Strive, Wait, and Pray.

STRIVE—yet I do not promise
  The prize you dream of to-day
Will not fade when you think to grasp it,
  And melt in your hand away;
But another and holier treasure,
  You would now perchance disdain,
Will come when your toil is over,
  And pay you for all your pain.

Wait—yet I do not tell you
  The hour you long for now,
Will not come with its radiance vanished,
  And a shadow upon its brow;
Yet far through the misty future,
  With a crown of starry light,
An hour of joy you know not,
  Is winging her silent flight.

Pray—though the gift you ask for
  May never comfort your fears—
May never repay your pleading,
  Yet pray with hopeful tears;
An answer—not that you long for,
  But diviner,—will come one day;
Your eyes are too dim to see it,
  Yet Strive, and Wait, and Pray.

Communion Hymn.

SAVIOUR, we take this cup,
  And this memorial bread,
In memory of that hour in which
  Thy blood for us was shed;
A simple act of love,
  We do it in Thy name;
And, as we thus obey Thy law,
  The promised blessing claim.

We worship not these types
  Of Thine abounding love;
We worship Thee, exalted One,
  Enthroned in heaven above.
The bread is still but bread;
  The wine is only wine.
No sacrifice is offered here;
  The sacrifice was Thine.

No Aaron stands beside
  The sacramental board;
Than Thee, we own no other *Priest*
  Or sacrifice, dear Lord.
No altar do we raise,
  Nor golden censer swing;
Our altar was without the camp,
  Thyself the offering.

We bring contrited hearts,
  And offer them to Thee;
Do thou accept the worthless gift,
  Thou "Lamb of Calvary."
Cleanse us from every stain,
  And make us truly Thine;
And, as we keep this sacred feast,
  Fill us with joy divine.

Unite our hearts to all
  Who run the Christian race;
Thy host baptismal—many-named—
  One host, through sovereign grace.
Let Thy constraining love
  To holy deeds incite,
And lead us all in love to live
  As "children of the light."

Let these memorials be
  Pledges of future bliss,
When we shall take at heaven's board
  A holier meal than this;
When we shall see Thy face,
  And bow before Thy throne,
Seeing without symbolic aids,
  Knowing as we are known.

M. B. Smith.

Passaic, N. J., October, 1863.

Love.

WHEN on the heart we look to find
  Whose cherished image it doth wear,
We learn that not the loftiest mind
  Doth grave its name most deeply there,
But the forgiving, true, and kind.
  And knowing this, and that above
All offerings that can rendered be
  To us, we most desire love,
It hath a marvel been to me,
  That gentleness and charity
We strive not harder to attain,
  Though for ourselves alone the gain.
Doth not a hasty spirit fling
  That one first drop of bitterness
Into love's pure and healing spring,
  That else would flow forth but to bless?
Or like an unquenched spark it lies
  E'en midst the gathered bonds of home;
It fires, it snaps the tender ties
  That should bind brethren into one.

Oh! for that calm and equal mind
  Whose peace a breath may not disturb;
Who, where the soil seems all unkind,
  Some hidden virtue still will find,
And its own enmity doth curb.

Few spots of earth have fruitless proved,
When patient hands have come to till;
Few hearts but some have justly loved,
Few but we may love if we will.
Are any pure? Hath Love a law
By which unmingled spotless worth,
Alone, may claim regard from her?
Then may she turn to-day from earth.

The trait to love must oft be sought,
Like veins in treasure-yielding ground;
If the bare surface holds it not,
Deeper, perchance, it may abound.
And having found it, Oh, how fair
The uncovered grace shows to the light!
The whole wide, stony waste doth wear
For it new beauty in our sight.
The gold is reached! Its hue we see!
All hid in our own breasts of such
As, by some secret alchemy,
Thrills at its first life-giving touch,
And glows with kindred sympathy!

"I shall be Satisfied."

NOT here! Not here! Not satisfied! wherever
Hope's joyous song is lost in sorrow's moan;
Not where anticipation's light hath never
On the fulfilment of its promise shone.

Not where the light from happy eyes is fading;
Where on each hearth the shadow of the bier
Falls darkly,—every home with gloom invading,
And chastening love itself with mortal fear.

Not where so many cold, harsh words are spoken;
Not where so few may breathe love's peaceful air;
Where cherished ties are in a moment broken,
And life's long agony becomes despair.

Not here,—where every dream of bliss deceives us,
Where the worn spirit never gains it goal;
Where, haunted ever by the thoughts that grieve us,
Across us floods of bitter memory roll.

Not here! Not here! Not where the sparkling waters
Fade into mocking sand as we draw near;
Where in the wilderness each footstep falters,—
I shall be satisfied! but oh! not here!

There is a land where every pulse is thrilling
With rapture, earth's sojourners may not know;
Where Heaven's repose the weary heart is stilling,
And peacefully life's time-tossed currents flow.

Ear hath not heard, nor hath eye seen the vision
Of light and loveliness beyond the skies;
Hope is forgotten there in full fruition,
And the heart vainly to conceive it tries.

Far out of sight, while yet the flesh enfolds us,
Lies the fair country where our hearts abide;
And of its bliss is naught more wondrous told us
Than these few words, "I shall be satisfied."

Satisfied? Satisfied?—the spirit's yearning
For sweet companionship with kindred minds;
The silent love that here meets no returning—
The inspiration which no language finds.

Shall they be satisfied? The soul's vague longings—
The aching void which nothing earthly fills—
Oh! what desires upon my soul are thronging,
As I look upward to the heavenly hills.

Thither my weak and weary steps are tending—
Saviour and Lord! with Thy frail child abide!
Guide me toward home, where, all my wanderings ending,
I shall see Thee, and "shall be satisfied."

R. A. R.

MOUNT HOLLY, November 19, 1852.

The Invitation.

"COME."—Matt. xi. 28.

I HAVE a Friend! a precious Friend, unchanging, wise, and true;
The chief among ten thousand!—Oh! I wish *you* knew Him too!
When all the woes that wait on me relax each feeble limb,
I know who waits to welcome me—have *you* a Friend like Him?
He comforts me—He strengthens me, how can I then repine?
He loveth *me!* This faithful Friend in life and death is mine.

I have a Father true and fond, He cares for all my needs;
His patience bore my faithless ways, my mad and foolish deeds;
To me He sends sweet messages,—He waiteth but to bless;—
Have you a Father like to mine, in such deep tenderness?
For me a kingdom doth He keep, for me a crown is won;
I was a rebel once—He calls the rebel child His son.

I have a proved, unerring Guide, whose love I often grieve;
He brings me golden promises my heart can scarce receive;
He leadeth me, and hope and cheer doth for my path provide;
For dreary nights and days of drought, have *you* so sure a Guide?
Quench not the faintest whisper that the heavenly Dove may bring,
He seeks with holy love to lure the wanderer 'neath His wing.

I have a Home — a Home *so* bright, its beauties none can know;
Its pavement sapphire, and such palms — none ever saw below.

Its golden streets resound with joy, its pearly
 gates with praise;
A temple standeth in the midst, no human hands
 could raise,
And there unfailing fountains flow, and pleasures
 never end;
Who makes that home so glorious? It is my
 loving Friend.

My Friend, my Father, and my Guide, and this
 our radiant home,
Are offered you — turn not away! *to-day* I pray
 you —" Come."
My Father yearns to welcome you,—His heart,
 His house to share;
My Friend is yours — my home is yours — my
 Guide will lead you there;
Behold One altogether fair—the faithful and the
 true,
He pleadeth with you for your love — He gave
 His life for *you.*

Oh! leave the worthless things you seek, they
 perish in a day;
Serve now the true and living God, from idols
 turn away.
Watch for the Lord, who comes to reign, enter
 the open door;

Give Him thine heart—thy broken heart—thou'lt
ask it back no more.
Trust Him for grace, and strength, and love, and
all thy troubles end—
Oh! come to Jesus! and you'll find in Him a
loving Friend.

Obedience.

"The cup which my Father hath given me, shall I not drink it."

DO ye not know—do ye not feel—
How much of earthly taint
Lingers around the human heart,
And makes the spirit faint?

How many a foolish, wrong desire
Doth lead the mind astray,
In the wide search for happiness
Far from the narrow way.

And even when the light of joy
Is beaming o'er the heart,
How few are guided, by its rays,
To choose the better part.

No! we forget, when all around
  Is smooth, and bright, and fair,
The Being who betows the good,
  And makes us all His care.

Aye! often-times forget, until
  He, who is wise and just,
Sends down His messengers of grief
  To prove our love and trust.

Then not for us—oh! 'not for us—
  To say what should be given
By Him, who knows how much we need,
  To turn our hearts to Heaven.

Rejected of Men.

"The foxes have holes, and the birds of the air have nests, but the Son of Man hath not where to lay his head." —*Matt.* viii. 20.

BIRDS have their quiet nest,
  Foxes their holes, and man his peaceful bed;
All creatures have their rest,
But Jesus had not where to lay his head.

Winds have their hour of calm—
And waves—to slumber on the voiceless deep;
Eve hath its breath of balm
To hush all senses and all sounds to sleep.

The wild deer hath its lair,
The homeward flocks the shelter of their shed;
All have their rest from care,
But Jesus had not where to lay his head.

And yet he came to give
The weary and the heavy laden rest—
To bid the sinner live,
And soothe our griefs to slumber on his breast.

What! then, am I, my God,
Permitted thus the paths of peace to tread?
Peace — purchased by the blood
Of Him who had not where to lay his head.

I—who once made him grieve;
I—who once bid his gentle spirit mourn—
Whose hands essayed to weave
For his meek brow the cruel crown of thorn:—

Oh! why should I have peace?
Why?—but for that unchanged, undying love,
Which would not—could not cease,
Until it made me heir of joys above.

Yes! but for pardoning grace,
I feel I never should in glory see
The brightness of that face,
That once was pale and agonized for me

Let the birds seek their nest,
Foxes their holes, and man his peaceful bed;
Come, Saviour, on my breast
Deign to repose thine oft-rejected head!

Come! give me rest, and take
The only rest on earth Thou lov'st—within
A heart, that for Thy sake
Lies bleeding, broken, penitent for sin.

The Love of Christ.

HOW hath he loved us?—ask the star
That, on its wondrous mission sped,
Hung trembling o'er that manger scene
Where He, the Eternal, bowed His head;
He, who of earth doth seal the doom,
Found in her lowliest inn—no room.

Judea's mountains,—lift your voice,
  Deep legends of his love to tell;
Thou favored Olivet,—so oft
  At prayerful midnights love so well,—
And Cedron's brook,—whose rippling wave
Frequent his wearied feet did lave.

How hath He loved us?—ask the band
  That fled his woes with faithless haste,—
Ask the weak friend's denial tone,
  Scarce by his bitterest tears effaced;
Ask of the traitor's kiss—and see
What Jesus hath endured for thee:—

Ask of Gethsemane,—whose dews
  Shrank from the moisture strangely red,
Which, in that unwatched hour of pain,
  His agonizing temples shed,—
The scourge, the thorn, whose anguish sore,
Like the unanswering lamb, he bore.

How hath He loved us?—ask the Cross,—
  The Roman spear, the shrouded sky;
Ask of the sheeted dead, who burst
  Their cerements at his fearful cry:—
Oh! ask no more!—but bow thy pride,
And yield thy heart to Him who died.

The Little Heart's-Ease.

A GARDENER went, one sunshiny day,
To look at his gay parterre;
To admire his flowers in their handsome array,
As with fragrance they scented the air:
And to walk in the shade of his stately trees,
That were waving their boughs in the morning breeze.

But, alas! alas! when he reached his ground,
What a scene of disorder and sadness he found!
Each beautiful flower was drooping its head,
And rapidly fading away;
And unnumbered fair leaves on the pathway were shed,
From the trees in their early decay:
And our gardener hastily sought for the reason,
Why this should have happened in spring's lovely season.

So he walked up first to his favorite Oak,
All withering, and asked it, "why?"
And the noble old tree thus mournfully spoke:—
"I thought I as well might die;

For I bear no fruit, nor with flowerets bloom,
And my awkward branches want so much room—
  I'm a clumsy and useless thing;
If I were a rose-tree, like that within reach,
Or if I had fruit like the soft, round peach,
  Some profit I then might bring;
But as I have nothing but leaves to give,
What motive have I for wishing to live?"

"Well, Lady Rose, with your sweet, open face,
  And cheeks of a delicate hue,
I had hoped that for months you my garden would grace,—
  Tell me, what is the matter with you?"
And the pretty Rose said, as she shook on her stem,
"Just look at your Oak trees; if I were like them,
  How happy and proud I should be!
I should rear my tall head in your well-cultured ground,
An ornament there, which for many miles round
  Admiring people might see;
But a poor little flower, unproductive as I,
What use is it to you?—I'd much rather die."

"Oh! beautiful Vine, which I trained with such care
  To climb up the sheltering wall;
Say, why are you trailing so dolefully there,
  And what has occasioned your fall?"

And the vine faintly murmured: "As I had not strength
My own weight to sustain, I determined at length
Not to trouble my friends any longer:
Could I yield a shade like the wide-spreading trees,
Or if, like the flowers, I had gifts that would please,
Why, then, I might try to grow stronger;
But a poor feeble creature, requiring a stay,
Had better make haste to get out of the way."

Quite saddened with looks and with words of gloom,
The gardener with joy espied
A dear little Heart's-ease, in full, rich bloom,
As fresh as a fair young bride:
It turned up its bright, little face toward him,
With a smile which none of its neighbors would dim;
And he said, with surprise, "How is it
That you so contented and healthful appear?
And that yours is the only countenance here,
That welcomes me in my visit?"
And the Heart's-ease replied, in a quick, cheerful tone,
"Dear master, I felt that I was not my own."

"And it seemed to my simple perception clear,
  That you certainly wanted me;
For you would have planted an acorn here,
  Had you wished for a stately tree;
Or had you desired sweet grapes to find,
A vine-plant would in my place have twined;
  And therefore, my obvious duty
Was to strive and grow with untiring zest,
Since the hearty endeavor to do one's best
  Is the truest worth and beauty;
And I saw that the work which you gave me
    to do,
Was to grow up a fine little Heart's-ease for you."

Dear reader! let this simple Heart's-ease teach
  The moral which I wish it to impart:
Sigh not for stations placed beyond thy reach,
  But strive to serve thy Maker where thou art:
The gardener soweth only tiny seeds
  Where he desires to raise but simple flowers;
If God required from thee an angel's deeds,
  He would have given thee an angel's powers;
But all he asks from each of us while here,
  Is, that with calm contentment we should rest
In our appointed and appropriate sphere,
  And there, with loving spirit, do our best.

Communion Hymn.

O LORD! how happy should we be,
If we could cast our care on thee;
If we from self could rest,
And feel at heart that one above,
In perfect wisdom, perfect love,
Is working for the best.

How far from this our daily life,
Ever disturbed by anxious strife,
By sudden, wild alarms
Oh, could we but relinquish all
Our earthly props, and simply fall
On thy Almighty arms!

Could we but kneel, and cast our load—
E'en while we pray—upon our God,
Then rise with lightened cheer;
Sure, that the Father, who is nigh
To still the famished raven's cry,
Will hear in that we fear.

We cannot trust Him as we should;
So chafes fallen nature's restless mood,
To cast its peace away;
Yet birds and flow'rets round us preach;
All, all the present evil teach,
Sufficient for the day.

Lord, make these faithless hearts of ours
Such lessons learn from birds and flowers;
  Make them from self to cease,
Leave all things to a Father's will,
And taste before Him, lying still
  E'en in affliction — peace!

Patience.

"Thy work this hour is Patience."

I HAD been mourning o'er my uselessness;
  I felt as if to me the words applied:
"Cut off, and withered like a branch," unless
  It could be proved occasion was denied,
By God's true wisdom, for activity;
  And visible deeds of the weak faith I had;
My idleness, enforced, was mystery,
  And my heart went in sackcloth clad.
Alas! it was self-will that made me blind
  To the deep, solemn truth I ought to know;
Then came to me an earnest voice, and kind,
  That bade me, "Work *his* work who laid
      low."
And when despairingly I said, "I would,
  If I but knew what God desired of me,"
The answer came to break my sullen mood:
"Let Patience have her perfect work in thee."

While still I mused on this reply, and sought
To test its truth and quiet comforting,
I chanced (as mortals say) to meet a thought
An earnest, poet heart had learned to sing.
'Twas the same lesson: to a dying man
A priest was summoned, and the penitent
Mourned the expiring of his active span,
And that his time for *work* for God was spent:
"*Thy work this hour is Patience!*" he returned,
And the vexed soul received the gracious word;
The mystery of "being still" he learned,
And when death called, the message calmly heard.
Oh! that upon my heart may be impressed
The humbling lesson which these few words tell;
Nor deem that "being patient" is a rest,
Or easy toil because invisible;
When I am tempted by the enemy
To murmur that my hands find nought to do—
When days, and weeks, and months pass heavily,
Bearing no record, to a human view;—
When e'en my mental powers seem asleep,
Or dulled, or wearied by my body's pain—
May I remember then the truth so deep:
"Thy work is Patience!" and no more complain;

Each hour comes singly; and with every hour
   Some duty, or some task, from God is sent:
Lord, give me resignation for my dower;
   With thy appointments make me still content;
And when my blind, imperfect spirit deems
   That unseen works are nothing in thy sight,
Recall me from the influence of such dreams;
   Nor with these phantom-shadows let me fight.
With due submission, Master, let me bear
   The humbling lot Thy wisdom hath ordained;
Teach me in it Thy lovely cross to share,
   By shameful scourging and defilement stained;
And, when I, suffering, seem to hang thereon,
   Thro' hours of silent inactivity,
Oh! let me hear Thy heart-inspiring tone:
"'Thy work this hour is Patience'—be like me!"
Without Thy gracious aid I cannot learn
   The mystery of my appointed task.
Oh! meek and lowly One, to Thee I turn,
   And help in this extremity I ask;
When my hour's work is Patience, teach me how
   It may be done most sure and perfectly;
So shall my ceaseless labor not allow
   Time for regrets and unreality.
Oh! Lord, imprint upon my inmost heart
   The Patience that doth work experience;—
The hope which maketh not ashamed impart,
   And raise me from the lower world of sense;

Give me my work and strength for every hour;
And by Thy Holy Spirit's touch, instil
The simple purpose (which is heavenly power,)
Of perfect resignation to Thy will!

After A Silent Meeting.

Written by a Lady—a member of the Society of Friends.

SILENT! then ye heard not
My beloved's greeting!
Knew not how we kept our tryst,
The parting, *and the meeting.*

Heard ye not my moaning
As I told my sorrow?
Nor His blessed words of hope,
"Joy cometh on the morrow?"

Heard ye not the whisper
Of my soul confessing?
Nor His faithful "I forgive,
Peace to thee, and blessing?"

Then, indeed, was silence!
Surely you could hear it,
With its low "amen! amen!"
Falling on my spirit.

The amen grew louder,
  Like an anthem pealing,
As it answered to the voice,
  All His will revealing.

Will—that I should suffer,
  Share His crown of sorrow!
Loving service give to-day,
  Reign with *him to-morrow!*

Heard ye that "To-morrow!"
  As the angels o'er us
Sang in hallelujahs loud
  The triumphant chorus?

Heard ye that "Forever!"
  As in holy vision
My beloved bore my soul
  Far to Faith's fruition?

Heard ye His low promise:
"Never will I leave thee;
Be thou faithful unto death;
  A crown of Life I give thee!"

Oh! then call not "silent,"
  Hours so full of singing!
Even now, from wall to wall,
  Hear the echoes ringing!

Looking off unto Jesus.

OH! eyes that are weary,
  And hearts that are sore,
Look off unto Jesus,
  And sorrow no more.
The light of His countenance
  Shineth so bright,
That on earth, as in heaven,
  There need be "no night."

Looking off unto Jesus,
  My eyes cannot see
The troubles and dangers
  That throng about me.
They cannot be blinded
  With sorrowful tears—
They cannot be shadowed
  With unbelief fears.

Looking off unto Jesus,
  My spirit is blest;
In the world I have turmoil,
  In Him I have rest.
The sea of my life
  All about me may roar,
When I look unto Jesus,
  I hear it no more.

Looking off unto Jesus,
  I go not astray;
My eyes are upon Him,
  And He shows me the way.
The path may seem dark
  As He leads me along,
But following Jesus
  I *cannot* go wrong.

Looking off unto Jesus,
  Oh! may I be found,
When the waters of Jordan
  Encompass me round;
Let them bear me away
  In His presence to be;
'Tis but seeing Him nearer,
  Whom always I see.

Then, then I shall know
  The full beauty and grace
Of Jesus, my Lord,
  When I stand face to face.
I shall know how His love
  Went before me each day,
And wonder that *ever*
  My eyes turned away.

Dying Grace.

WHEN from disease or weariness,—
I know not which—weak, in distress,
I on my couch am laid,
How sweet it is, while waiting there,
Released from all disturbing care,
To feel my peace is made!

I seem escaped from earthly things,
Loosed by that Spirit's power, who brings
The suppliant near the throne;
While sins that threatened me before,
Now silenced, terrify no more,
And nought but love is known.

The dark clouds that I feared might lower
And fill with gloom my final hour,
Have from this spot passed by:
Lo! where I forward looked with dread,
I now, midst fruits and flowers am led
Beneath a cloudless sky!

'Tis not by process of the mind,
By thought, by argument, I find
From all fear this release:
But as the showers do silent fall
Where they are sent, without my call
Comes down this perfect peace.

Oft have I wrestled in my day
When strength was mine, and all my way
  Seemed strewed with hinderance:
And oft my cup seemed running o'er
With answers given, but ne'er before
  Found I such peace as this!

In perfect weakness, when I feel
No earthly balm my wounds could heal,
  And none from heaven be sought;
Then all my bruises are made whole,
While to my drooping, fainting soul,
  Cordials of joy are brought.

Ah! 'tis not yet my time to die;
This hour of languor shall pass by:
  'Tis but of toil my pain!
When these tired limbs their couch have pressed,
I, rising soon, refreshed by rest,
  Will seek my task again.

But never more will I forget
The Saviour I this day have met
  In Love-divine's embrace.
When fears of death assert their power,
I'll answer, with the dying hour,
  He will bring dying grace!

Praying in Spirit.

Matthew vi. 6.

I NEED not leave the jostling world,
  Or wait till daily tasks are o'er,
To fold my palms in secret prayer,
  Within the close-shut closet door.

There is a viewless cloistered room,
  As high as Heaven, as fair as day;
Where, though my *feet* may join the throng,
  My *soul* can enter in, and pray.

When I have banished wayward thoughts,
  Of sinful works the fruitful seed,—
When folly wins my ear no more,
  The closet door is shut, indeed!

No human step approaching, breaks
  The blissful stillness of the place;
No shadow steals across the light
  That falls from my Redeemer's face!

And never, through those crystal walls,
  The clash of life can pierce its way;
Nor ever can a human ear
  Drink in the spirit words I say.

One hearkening, even cannot know
  When I have crossed the threshold o'er,
For He alone, who hears my prayer,
  Has heard the shutting of the door.

HARRIET M. KIMBALL.

Look for the Flowers.

HERE we, earth's wanderers,
    Timid and brave,
Hasten with onward step
    Nearer the grave;
And, in our pilgrimage,
    Should we not see
All that is beautiful,
    Lovesome, and free?
Should we, with sullen hand,
    Gather the thorn?
Should we, with murmuring heart,
    Sit all forlorn?
Should we, in rambling
    Over the meads,
Look but for pestilent,
    Poisonous weeds?

Should we not, joyously,
Hand locked in hand,
A hopeful, a jubilant,
Brotherly band,
Look for the flowers?

In the far nooks of life,
In the deep shade,
Where, amidst evil things,
Good well might fade,
God sends the sunny beam,
God sends the showers,
Nursing humanity's
Ever bright flowers;
Sin may be rife enough,
But the good part
Lieth low, hidden in
Every heart.
God sent the stream at first
From His own fount;
Christ, in diffusing it,
Died on the mount;
And, amidst stony ways,
Ripples are heard,
Like the half-uttered notes
Of a low bird;

Dark tho' the fate of us,
That matters not;
In the glad soul of us
Lives the bright spot:
Look for the flowers!

Are they not sainted ones,
Graciously given,
Who in their gentle hand,
Lead us to heaven?
When they return to us
In the dim night,
Are they not angel-like,
Holy and bright?
Sanctified, purified
Unto us now,
With a heaven-garland
Encircling each brow?
Turn to the living ones;
Then, as they stand,
Touch the live hearts of them
With thy love wand
Seek not the weeds in them,
And, to thy sight,
They will be angel-like,
Holy and bright:
Look for the flowers!

Look for the flowery way,
Life has its clouds,—
Treasured ones suddenly
Wrapped in their shrouds;
Hope often dashed aside,
Hearts rudely torn,
And o'er wrecked promises
Oft do we mourn;
Hints too are given us,
That our swift day,
Rapidly, rapidly
Fleeteth away.
Up, then, and cheerfully!
Trust me, there lies
Much that is beautiful
'Neath the broad skies.
Go on life's pilgrimage,
Hand locked in hand,
A hopeful, a jubilant,
Brotherly band,
Looking for flowers;

Delay of Christian Effort.

STRIVING in coward listlessness
  Each good work still to shun,
How can a Father's sanction bless
  Our labors ne'er begun?

Go boldly up—each hind'rance meet—
  Assail that nearest by;
When duty calls, to bear defeat
  Is better than to fly!

How know'st thou, but th' occasion rare,
  This very hour supplies?
A victim struggles in the snare;
  A brother, captive lies.

He, who the search unwearied keeps,
  With fervent, zealous mind,
May rescue some; but he who sleeps,
  Surely no souls shall find.

Time will not fold, for thee, its wings;
  Onward thy steps are pressed;
Slothful and diligent it brings
  Where both, alike, must rest.

If it be sweet, when day is past,—
  Though not increased thy store—
To think, not to th' endeavor lost
  Its fruitless moments were.

How sweeter far will be at length,
  As wanes life's setting sun,
The thought to Christ was given its strength,
  Though nought but heaven be won!

The Sun of Righteousness.

SHADOW of death! on thy valley of sadness
  Beams of the morning are shedding their light;
Gilding thy caverns with glory and gladness,
  Chasing the fears and the phantoms of night.

Long have thy victims in apathy slumbered,
  Or poured their despair through a fathomless gloom;
But the days of their doubt and their darkness are numbered;
  No more shall the earth be a type of the tomb.

No more shall the heart cry in vain for a pillow
To lull its faint hope, like a motherless child;
No more shall the mind, like the dove o'er the billow,
Traverse in despondence a shelterless wild.

The last star has set, and the Sun, in his splendor,
From the chambers of day in his majesty springs!
And a gold-dropping glory, by mercy made tender,
Distils on the faint from his far-spreading wings!

He comes in his grace, and he comes in his beauty,
To brighten man's darkest and drearest abode;
To shine on the fields and the deserts of duty,—
To light up the pathway that leads us to God.

Behold! how his rays on the mountains are sparkling!
The shadows of midnight are lost to our view.
Shout, nations! no more shall you wander all darkling;
For the "Light of the world" beameth brightly on you.

He will light you through toil, he will light you
through sorrow;
He will beam on your journey, and smile on
your grave;
He will wake up your souls to an unsetting mor-
row;
For the "Light of the world" is all-powerful
to save!

I will Lead Them.

"I will lead them in paths they have not known."—*Isaiah* xlii. 16.

LEAD, Saviour, lead; amid the encircling
gloom
Lead Thou me on.
The night is dark, and I am far from home;
Lead Thou me on.
Keep Thou my feet; I do not ask to see
The distant scene—one step enough for me.

I was not ever thus, nor pray'd that Thou
Should'st lead me on:
I loved to choose and see my path; but now,
Lead Thou me on.
I loved the glare of day; and, spite of fears,
Pride ruled my will:—Remember not past years!

So long thy power hath bless'd me—sure it still
Will lead me on,
O'er vale and hill, through stream and torrent, till
The night is gone,
And with the morn, those angel-faces smile,
Which I have loved long since, and lost awhile.

Thy Way—not Mine.

THY way—not *mine*, O Lord,
However dark it be!
Lead me by Thine own hand;
Choose out the path for me.

Smooth let it be, or rough,
It will be still the best;
Winding or straight, it matters not,
It leads me to thy rest.

I dare not choose my lot;
I would not, if I might:
Choose Thou for me, my God,
So shall I walk aright.

The kingdom that I seek
  Is Thine; so let the way
That leads to it be Thine,
  Else surely I might stray.

Take Thou my cup, and it
  With joy or sorrow fill!
As best to Thee may seem,
  Choose Thou my good and ill.

Choose Thou for me my friends,
  My sickness, or my health;
Choose Thou my cares for me,
  My poverty or wealth.

Not mine—not mine the choice,
  In things or great or small;
Be Thou my guide, my strength,
  My wisdom, and my all.

Over the River.

OVER the river they beckon to me,
  Loved ones who've crossed to the further side;
The gleam of their snowy robes I see,
  But their voices are lost in the dashing tide.

There's one with ringlets of sunny gold,
And eyes the reflection of heaven's own blue;
He crossed in the twilight, gray and cold,
And the pale mist hid him from mortal view.
We saw not the angels who met him there,
The gates of the city we could not see,
Over the river—over the river—
My brother stands waiting to welcome me.

Over the river the boatman pale
Carried another, the household pet;
Her brown curls waved in the gentle gale—
Darling Minnie! I see her yet.
She crossed on her bosom her dimpled hands,
And fearlessly entered the phantom bark,
We felt it glide from the silver sands,
And all our sunshine grew strangely dark.
We know she is safe on the further side,
Where all the ransomed and angels be;
Over the river—the mystic river—
My childhood's idol is waiting for me.

For none return from those quiet shores
Who cross with the boatman cold and pale—
We hear the dip of the golden oars,
And catch a gleam of the snowy sail:

And lo! they have passed from our yearning hearts,
Who cross the stream, and are gone for aye,
We may not sunder the veil apart,
That hides from our vision the gates of day;
We only know that their barks no more
May sail with us over life's stormy sea;
Yet somewhere, I know, on the unseen shore,
They watch, and beckon, and wait for me.

And I sit and think when the sunset's gold
Is flushing river and hill and shore,
I shall one day stand by the water cold,
And list for the sound of the boatman's oar;
I shall watch for a gleam of the flapping sail,
I shall hear the boat as it gains the strand,
I shall pass from sight with the boatman pale,
To the better shore of the spirit land;
I shall know the loved who have gone before,
And joyfully sweet will the meeting be,
When over the river—the peaceful river—
The angel of death shall carry me.

Leave the Future.

"LEAVE the future"—let it rest
  Simply on thy Saviour's will;
"Leave the future"—they are blest
  Who, confiding, hoping still,
    Trust his mercy
To preserve them safe from ill.

Thus, like travellers in the dark,
  Following the appointed way,
Though no beacon-fire they mark,
  Still their faithful spirits say,
    "We will follow—
Jesus leads to perfect day."

Let the present moment pass
  With a blessing on its head;
And as time metes out his glass,
  While our sands are numbered
    Use the present—
Soon 'twill sleep with ages fled.

When with mists thy joys are clouded,
  And when darkness fills the air—
When with sin thy soul is shrouded—
  Then to Calvary repair;
    Jesus gives thee
Beams of pure refulgence there.

Hymn.

I JOURNEY through a desert drear and wild,
Yet is my heart by such sweet thoughts beguiled,
Of Him on whom I lean—my strength and stay,
I can forget the sorrows of the way.

Thoughts of His love! the root of every grace,
Which finds in this poor heart a dwelling-place;
The sunshine of my soul, than day more bright,
And my calm pillow of repose by night.

Thoughts of His sojourn in this vale of tears!
The tale of love unfolded in those years
Of sinless suffering, and patient grace,
I love again, and yet again, to trace.

Thoughts of His glory! on the cross I gaze,
And there behold its sad, yet healing rays;
Beacon of hope, which, lifted up on high,
Illumes with heavenly light the tear-dimm'd eye.

Thoughts of His coming! for that joyful day
In patient hope I watch, and wait, and pray;
The dawn draws nigh — the midnight shadows flee;
Oh, what a sunrise will that advent be!

Thus while I journey on, my Lord to meet,
My thoughts and meditations are so sweet,
Of Him on whom I lean—my strength, my stay,
I can forget the sorrows of the way.

M. J. D.

A Word.

I HAVE known one word hang starlike
  O'er a weary waste of years,
And it only shone the brighter
  Looked at through a mist of tears;
While a weary wanderer gathered
  Hope and heart on life's dark way,
By its faithful promise shining
  Clearer day by day.

I have known a spirit calmer
  Than the calmest lake, and clear
As the heavens that gazed upon it,
  With no wave of hope or fear;
But the storm had swept across it,
  And its deepest depths were stirred,
Never, never more to slumber,
  Only by a word.

I have known a word more gentle
  Than the breath of summer air,
In a listening heart it nestled,
  And it lived forever there.
Not the beating of its prison
  Stirred it every night or day;
Only with the heart's last throbbing
  Could it pass away.

Words are mighty, words are living;
  Serpents with their venomed stings,
Or bright angels, crowding round us
  With heaven's light upon their wings;
Every word has its own spirit,
  True or false, that never dies;
Every word man's lips have uttered
  Lives on record in the skies.

HOUSEHOLD WORDS.

Come unto Me.

WITH tearful eyes I look around;
  Life seems a dark and stormy sea;
Yet 'midst the gloom I hear a sound—
  A heavenly whisper, "Come to Me!"

It tells me of a place of rest;
  It tells me where my soul may flee:—
Oh! to the weary, faint, oppress'd,
  How sweet the bidding, "Come to Me!"

When the poor heart with anguish learns
  That earthly props resigned must be,
And from each broken cistern turns
  It hears the accents, "Come to Me!"

When against sin I strive in vain,
  And cannot from its yoke get free,
Sinking beneath the heavy chain,
  The words arrest me, "Come to Me!"

When nature shudders, loth to part
  From all I love, enjoy, or see;
When a faint chill steals o'er my heart,
  A sweet voice utters, "Come to Me!"

Come, for all else must fade and die;
  Earth is no resting-place for thee;
Heavenward direct thy weeping eye,—
  I am thy Portion, "Come to Me!"

Oh, voice of mercy, voice of love!
  In conflict, grief, and agony,
Support me, cheer me from above,
  And gently whisper, "Come to me!"

The Safe Refuge.

"Come unto me all ye that labor and are heavy laden."

ART thou weary? art thou languid?
Art thou sore distrest?
"Come unto Me," saith One, "and, coming,
Be at rest."

Hath He marks to lead me to Him,
If He be my Guide?
"In His feet and hands are wound-prints,
And his side."

Is there diadem, as monarch,
That His brow adorns?
"Yea, a crown in very 'surety,
But of thorns!"

If I find Him—if I follow,
What is guerdon here?
"Many a sorrow, many a labor,
Many a tear."

If I still hold closely to Him,
What hath He at last?
"Sorrow vanquished, labor ended,
Jordan past!"

If I ask Him to receive me,
Will He say me nay?
"Not till earth, not till heaven
Pass away!"

Tending, following, keeping, struggling,
Is He sure to bless?
"Angels, martyrs, prophets, pilgrims,
Answer, 'Yes.'"

Weary and Heavy Laden.

I HEARD the voice of Jesus say,
"Come unto me and rest;
Lay down, thou weary one, lay down
Thy head upon my breast."
I came to Jesus as I was,
Weary, and worn, and sad;
I found in Him a resting-place,
And He has made me glad.

I heard the voice of Jesus say,
"Behold, I freely give
The living water, thirsty one,
Stoop down and drink, and live."
I came to Jesus, and I drank
Of that life-giving stream;
My thirst was quenched, my soul revived,
And now I lived in Him.

I heard the voice of Jesus say,
"I am this dark world's light;
Look unto me, thy moon shall rise,
And all the day be bright."
I look'd to Jesus, and I found
In Him my star, my sun;
And in that light of life I'll walk
Till travelling days are done.

The Pilgrim.

"I SAW an aged Pilgrim,
Whose toilsome march was o'er,
With slow and painful footstep
Approaching Jordan's shore:
He first his dusty vestment
And sandals cast aside,
Then, with an air of transport,
Enter'd the swelling tide.

"I thought to see him shudder,
As cold the waters rose,
And fear'd lest o'er him, surging,
The murky stream should close;
But calmly and unshrinking,
The billowy path he trod,
And, cheer'd with Jesus' presence,
Pass'd o'er the raging flood.

"On yonder shore to greet him,
I saw a shining throng;
Some just begun their praising,
Some had been praising long;
With joy they bade him welcome,
And struck their harps again,
While through the heavenly arches
Peal'd the triumphal strain.

"Now in a robe of glory,
And with a starry crown,
I see the weary pilgrim
With Kings and Priests sit down;
With Prophets, Patriarchs, Martyrs,
And Saints, a countless throng,
He chants his great deliverance,
In never-ceasing song."*

Death.

WHERE shall I die? Shall death's cold hand
Arrest my breath, while dear ones stand
In silent, watchful love, to shed
Their tears around my quiet bed?

* American.—*Anon.*

Or shall I meet my final doom
Far from my country and my home?
Lord, to Thy will I bend the knee,
Thou evermore hast cared for me.

"*How* shall I die? Shall death's stern yoke
Subdue me by a single stroke?
Or shall my fainting frame sustain
The tedious languishing of pain?
Sinking in weariness away,
Slowly and sadly, day by day?
Lord, I repose my cares on thee—
Thou evermore hast cared for me.

"*When* shall I die? Shall death's stern call
Soon come my spirit to appal?
Or shall I live through circling years
A pilgrim in this vale of tears,
Surveying those I loved the best,
Who in the peaceful churchyard rest?
Lord, I await Thy wise decree;
Thou evermore hast cared for me."

On a Domestic Bereavement.

"Jesus wept."
"I am the resurrection and the life."—*John* xi.

THOU! who art touch'd with feeling of our woes,
Let me on thee my heavy burden cast!
My aching, anguish'd heart on thee repose,
Leaving with thee the sad, mysterious past;
Let me submissive bow, and kiss the rod;
Let me "be still, and know that thou art God."

Why should my harass'd, agitated mind,
Go round and round this terrible event?
Striving in vain some brighter side to find,
Some cause why all this anguish has been sent?
Do I indeed that sacred truth believe,
Thou dost not willingly afflict and grieve?

Infinite wisdom! can it ever err?
Infinite love! can it to us work ill:
Good, only good, dost thou, my God, confer,
Tho' it to me, alas! seem evil still:
Oh! let not finite, frail, presumptuous man,
Thine acts arraign—thy hidden purpose scan.

Oh! pity me, all crush'd beneath the blow,
  Thus weeping o'er this sad, mysterious blight;
My garden's richest, fairest plant laid low,
  Gemm'd with its dewy blossoms sparkling bright;
Just when its roseate blooms were set for fruit,
Stricken and shatter'd at the very root.

There are none like it left, and earth appears
  So stripp'd, so desolate, without its charms,
A barren waste, a mournful vale of tears,
  That, were I not supported by thine arms,
My pitying Saviour! this poor heart would break!
Oh! shield—oh! comfort, for thy mercy's sake.

My lovely gourd is wither'd in an hour!
  I droop, I faint, beneath the scorching sun:
My shepherd, lead me to some sheltering bower—
  There, where thy little flock "lie down at noon;"
Tho' of my dearest earthly joy bereft,
Thou art my portion still—thou, thou, my God, art left!

The Chastened Spirit.

"If ye endure chastening, God dealeth with you as with sons."—*Heb.* xii. 7.

OH, CHEER thee, cheer thee, suffering saint!
Though worn with chastening, be not faint!
And though thy night of pain seem long,
Cling to thy Lord—in him be strong;
He marks, he numbers every tear;
Not one faint sigh escapes his ear.

Oh, cheer thee, cheer thee! he has traced
Thy track through life, from first to last;
Each stage—the present, childhood, youth,
Has borne fresh witness to that truth,
Which soon will tune thy harp above,
"Loved with an everlasting love."

Then cheer thee, cheer thee! though the flame
Consume thy wasting, suffering frame;
Thy gold no harm shall find, nor loss;
He will but purge away the dross,
And fit it, graced with many a gem,
To form his glorious diadem.

Yes, *He will* cheer thee—he will prove,
The soul, encircled by his love,
Can meekly, midst its anguish, say,—
"Still will I trust him, though he slay!"
And he will make his words thine own—
"Father! thy will, not mine, be done."

The Exile.

MY soul, amid this stormy world,
Is like some flutter'd dove;
And fain would be as swift of wing
To flee to him I love.

The cords that bound my heart to earth
Were broken by his hand;
Before his cross I found myself
A stranger in the land.

That visage marr'd, those sorrows deep,
The vinegar and gall,
Were Jesus' golden chains of love
His captive to enthrall.

My heart is with him on his throne,
And ill can brook delay;
Each moment listening for the voice—
"Rise up, and come away."

With hope deferr'd, oft sick and faint,
"Why tarries he?" I cry;
And should the Saviour chide my haste,
Then would I make reply—

"May not an exile, Lord, desire
His own sweet land to see?
May not a captive seek release—
A pris'ner to be free?

"A child, when far away, may long
For home and kindred dear;
And she that waits her absent Lord,
May sigh till he appear.

"I would, my Lord and Saviour, know
That which no measure knows;
Would search the mystery of thy love,
The depth of all thy woes.

"I fain would strike my golden harp
Before the Father's throne—
There cast my crown of righteousness,
And sing what grace hath done.

"Ah! leave me not in this dark world
A stranger still to roam;
Come, Lord, and take me to thyself,
'Come, Jesus, quickly come.'"

The Harvest-Home.

"That both he that soweth, and he that reapeth, may rejoice together."—*John* iv. 36.

FROM the far-off fields of earthly toil,
  A goodly host they come,
And sounds of music are on the air,—
  'Tis the song of the Harvest-home.
The weariness and the weeping—
  The darkness has all pass'd by,
And a glorious sun has risen—
  The sun of Eternity!

We've seen those faces in days of yore,
  When the dust was on their brow,
And the scalding tear upon their cheek:
  Let us look at the laborers now!
We think of the life-long sorrow,
  And the wilderness days of care;
We try to trace the tear-drops,
  But no scars of grief are there.

There's a mystery of soul-chasten'd joy
  Lit up with sun-light hues,
Like morning flowers, most beautiful
  When wet with midnight dews.

There are depths of earnest meaning
  In each true and trustful gaze,
Telling of wondrous lessons
  Learnt in their pilgrim days.

And a conscious confidence of bliss,
  That shall never again remove,—
All the faith and hope of journeying years,
  Gather'd up in that look of love.
The long waiting days are over;
  They've received their wages now;
For they've gazed upon their Master,
  And His name is on their brow.

They've seen the safely garner'd sheaves,
  And the song has been passing sweet,
Which welcomed the last in-coming one
  Laid down at their Saviour's feet.
Oh! well does His heart remember,
  As those notes of praise sweep by,
The yearning, plaintive music
  Of earth's sadder minstrelsy.

And well does *He* know each chequer'd tale,
  As he looks on the joyous band—
All the lights and shadows that cross'd their path,
  In the distant pilgrim land;—

The heart's unspoken anguish—
  The bitter sighs and tears—
The long, long hours of watching—
  The changeful hopes and fears!

One had climb'd the rugged mountain-side;
  'Twas a bleak and wintry day;
The tempest had scatter'd his precious seed,
  And he wept as he turn'd away.
But a stranger-hand had water'd
  That seed on a distant shore,
And the laborers now are meeting
  Who never had met before.

And *one*—he had toil'd 'mid burning sands,
  When the scorching sun was high:
He had grasp'd the plough with a fever'd hand,
  And then laid him down to die:
But another, and yet another,
  Had fill'd that deserted field,
Nor vainly the seed they scatter'd,
  Where a brother's care had till'd.

Some with eager step went boldly forth,
  Broad-casting o'er the land;
Some water'd the scarcely budding blade,
  With a tender, gentle hand.

There's *one*—her young life was blighted
  By the withering touch of woe;
Her days were sad and weary,
  And she never went forth to sow;

But there rose from her lonely couch of pain,
  The fervent, pleading prayer;
She looks on many a radiant brow,
  And she reads the answers there!
Yes! sowers and reapers are meeting;
  A rejoicing host they come!
Will you join the echoing chorus?—
  'Tis the song of the Harvest-home!

The Divine Command.

I HEARD my Saviour say, the other morn,
  "Child, hast thou any meat?"
I answered, "No!" for I had toiled forlorn,
  And found no food to eat.

He stood beside me in the twilight dim,
  So that I scarce could see;
Yet by his care and voice, I knowing him,
  My heart beat joyously.

He bade me cast my weary, empty net
  Down on another side;
The waves were rich, my table soon was set,
  And I was satisfied.

Since then I fish not blindly,
  But ever turn unto the nearest brink;
When He *hearing* the thoughts which towards
    Him yearn,
  Gives more than I can think.

Oh! Master! Saviour! Guardian! Friend!
  And more than any earth-names tell;
Oh! ever let me see Thee on yon shore;
  Till there with Thee I dwell!

Abiding in Christ.

CHRISTIAN, wouldst thou *fruitful* be?
  Jesus says, "*Abide in me;*"
From him all thy fruit is found;
May it to his praise abound!

Christian, wouldst thou *holy* be?
Jesus says, "*Abide in me;*"
Sanctified in him thou art;
Sanctify him in thy heart.

Christian, wouldst thou *happy* be?
Jesus says, "*Abide in me;*"
He is thine exceeding joy—
Bliss divine! without alloy.

Christian, this thy motto be—
Jesus says, "*Abide in me;*"
Grace and strength from him receive—
As a branch in Jesus live.

Christian, him thou soon shalt see;
Then he'll say, "*Abide with me:*
"In my Father's house above—
In the bosom of His love."

"Whose am I?"

"'TIS *a point I long to know,*
Oft it causes anxious thought:
Do I love the Lord or no?
Am I his, or am I not?"

REPLY.

Mourner, why these anxious fears?
Wherefore shouldst thou doubtful be?
Christ, thine advocate, appears—
He has died instead of thee;
He thy punishment has borne—
Look to Jesus!—Cease to mourn!

"If I love, why am I thus?
Why this cold, this lifeless frame?
Hardly, sure, can they be worse,
Who have never heard his name!"

REPLY.

Frames and feelings fluctuate;
These thy saviour ne'er can be;
Love itself may oft abate;—
Learn thyself *in Christ* to see:
Then be *feelings* what they will,
Jesus is thy Saviour still!

The Divine Presence.

"There I will meet with thee, and I will commune with thee from above the mercy-seat."—*Exodus* xxv. 22.

WHEN to my closet I repair,
To breathe my soul's desires in prayer,
And, bending low at Jesus' feet,
I look towards the mercy-seat,
This promise, Lord, shall be my plea—
There, sinner, I will meet with thee.

When Holy Scripture I peruse,
And o'er its sacred pages muse,
Oh! then this precious word fulfil;
And while I seek to learn Thy will,
Draw near, in answer to my prayer,
And, gracious Saviour, meet me *there.*

When in Thy temple-courts I stand
Amid Thy little chosen band,
Assist me then my soul to raise
In earnest prayer and cheerful praise:
There let me Thy salvation see,
And, gracious Saviour, meet with me.

Or should it be Thy wise decree
To lay Thy chastening hand on me,
And make the couch of suffering mine,
Yet would Thy servant not repine,
If only this my portion be,
My Saviour! *there* to meet with Thee.

When sorrow's gloomy path I tread,
And threatening clouds meet o'er my head,
I'll onward go without a fear,
If only Jesus' voice I hear:
Even then the darkness light shall be,
If *there* my Saviour meet with me.

And when my closing hour draws nigh—
That solemn hour when I shall die—
When Jordan's banks I shall descend,
Leaving behind each earthly friend,
To Canaan's shores my spirit bear,
And, gracious Saviour! meet me *there.*

The Germs of the Beautiful.

SCATTER the germs of the beautiful
By the wayside let them fall,
That the rose may spring by the cottage gate,
And the vine on the garden wall.
Cover the rough and the rude of earth
With a veil of leaves and flowers,
And mark with the opening bud and cup
The march of summer hours.

Scatter the germs of the beautiful
In the holy shrines of home:
Let the pure, and the fair, and the graceful there,
In their loveliest lustre come;
Leave not a trace of deformity
In the temple of the heart;
But gather about its hearth the gems
Of Nature and of Art.

Scatter the germs of the beautiful
  In the temple of our God —
The God who starr'd the uplifted sky,
  And flower'd the trampled sod.
When he built a temple for himself,
  And a home for his priestly race,
He rear'd each arch in symmetry,
  And curved each line in grace.

Scatter the germs of the beautiful
  In the depths of the human soul:
They shall bud, and blossom, and bear the fruit,
  While the endless ages roll.
Plant with the flowers of charity
  The portals of the tomb,
And the fair and the pure above thy path
  In Paradise shall bloom.

The Loved and Lost.

"The loved and lost!" why do they call them lost,
  Because we miss them from our onward road?
God's unseen angel, o'er our pathway crossed,
Looked on us all, and loving them the most,
  Straightway relieved them from life's weary load.

They are not lost: they are within the door
  That shuts out loss, and every hurtful thing—
With angels bright, and loved ones gone before,
In their Redeemer's presence evermore,
  And God himself their Lord, and Judge, and King.

And this we call a "loss;"—Oh, selfish sorrow
  Of selfish hearts! Oh, we of little faith!
Let us look round, some argument to borrow
Why we in patience should await the morrow
  That surely must succeed this night of death.

Ay, look upon this dreary desert path,
  The thorns and thistles whereso'er we turn;
What trials and what tears, what wrongs and wrath!
What struggles and what strife the journey hath!
  They have escaped from these, and lo! we mourn.

Ask the poor sailor, when the wreck is done,
  Who with his treasures strove the shore to reach;
While with the raging waves he battled on,
Was it not joy where every joy seemed gone,
  To see his loved ones landed on the beach?

A poor wayfarer, leading by the hand
  A little child, had halted by the well
To wash from off her feet the clinging sand,
And tell the tired boy of that bright land
  Where, this long journey passed, they longed to dwell;

When lo! the Lord, who many mansions had,
  Drew near, and looked upon the suffering twain,
Then pitying spake, "Give me the little lad:
In strength renewed, and glorious beauty clad,
  I'll bring him with me when I come again."

Did she make answer selfishly and wrong—
  "Nay, but the woes I feel he too must share!"
Oh! rather, bursting into grateful song,
She went her way rejoicing, and made strong
  To struggle on, since he was freed from care.

We will do likewise: death hath made no breach
  In love and sympathy, in hope and trust;
No outward sign or sound our ears can reach,
But there's an inward, spiritual speech,
  That greets us still, though mortal tongues be dust.

It bids us do the work that they laid down;
  Take up the song where they broke off the
    strain;
So journeying till we reach the heavenly town,
Where are laid up our treasures and our crown,
  And our lost loved ones will be found again.

Following Jesus.

"O, send out Thy light and Thy truth: let them lead me: let them bring me unto Thy holy hill."—*Psalm* xliii. 3.

ACHE on, poor stricken heart, ache on;
  Thy Saviour's heart hath ach'd before:
It is thy precious benison
    To bear,—*He* bore!

Thy little cross of pain,—how light
  Compar'd with that, my soul, *He* knew!
Thy little ills and cares,—how slight,
    How nameless,—few!

Oh! had this life, like summer day,
  Shone brightly, soul! upon thy path,
From God thou long hadst staid away,
    A child of wrath.

But now, a drooping, trembling thing,
  Oft sorely smitten by His rod,
Thou comest, in thy griefs, to cling
          Closer to God.

Yet, aching, suffering heart, be still;
  Soon, soon shall life's short pang be o'er;
With its last pain it soon shall thrill,
          Then—feel no more.

Then feel no more?—Ah, no! Ah, no!
  Then feel but peace and bliss alone;
Then feel what angels feel—then know
          Their joys, its own.

Oh! that it now might rise, and win
  That conquest still to conflict given,
And garner up its hopes within
          Its God—its heaven.

Live sweetly with the holy dead,
  Their presence know,—their spirit share;
Think of their bliss—their pathway tread,
          Their image bear.

Oh, thus, with Jesus by thy side,
  What, what are earth's low griefs to thee?
Up then! in God's high strength abide,
          In Him, be free!

"The Secret of the Lord."

PSALMS XXV. 14.

BEHOLD, a pilgrim journeying on
  Through the maze of earth;
His staff his prop to lean upon,
  Unknown his place of birth.
Ask whence the smiles you see him wear
"The secret of the Lord" is there.

Behold the traveller on his way,
  Eyeing each scene around,
Deaf to each voice that bids him stay,
  Fast speeding o'er the ground.
Ask what his errand is, and where—
"The secret of the Lord" is there!

Behold him weary, sick, and poor,
  Yet pressing onward still;
Each trial patiently endure,
  And gain each toilsome hill.
Bid him his source of strength declare—
"The secret of the Lord" is there!

Tell him the few he used to meet,—
  Dearer than aught below,—
Have gather'd up their wearied feet,
  And quitted life's frail show.
Ask whence his calm and chasten'd air—
"The secret of the Lord" is there.

Go see him on his dying bed,
  Witness his gasping breath;
He talks of blood on Calvary shed,
  And says, "How sweet is death!"
Bestows his blessing, mounts—oh! where?
"The secret of the Lord" is there!

"I Am."

Exodus iii. 14.

WHEN God would teach mankind his name,
He calls himself the great "I Am;"
And leaves a blank where Christians may
Insert those things for which they pray.

The meaning is, as if He said,
"I Am" thy life, though thou be dead;
If thou art weak, thou need'st not fear,
"I Am" thy help, and I am near.

Dost thou because of sin repine?
"I Am" thy God, who saves from sin;
Although thy footsteps wandering rove,
Come, taste my mercy—"I Am" love.

If thou art dark, "I Am" thy light;
If thou art blind, "I Am" thy sight;
And when distress'd, "I Am," indeed,
A present help in time of need.

Art thou compell'd to take the field
Against thy foes, "I am thy shield
And thine exceeding great reward:"
Depend on me—"I Am" the Lord.

And art thou e'er disturbed in mind,
Look unto me, for "I Am" kind.
Hast thou e'er felt my chast'ning rod,
Be still, and know that "I Am" God.

I am to those who on me call,
Their Lord, their Saviour, and their all;
Their consolation, and their peace—
"I Am" the Lord their Righteousness.

The Desired Haven.

"Lord, now lettest Thou Thy servant depart in peace, according to Thy word."—*Luke* ii. 29.

"LORD, the waves are breaking o'er me and
around;
Oft of coming tempests I hear the moaning
sound;
Here there is no safety, rocks on either hand;
'Tis a foreign roadstead, a strange and hostile
land.
Wherefore should I linger? Others, gone before,
Long since safe are landed on a calm and friendly
shore;
Now the sailing orders, in mercy, Lord, bestow—
Loose the cable, let me go!

"Lord, the night is closing round my feeble
bark;
How shall I encounter its watches long and
dark?
Sorely worn, and shattered by many a billow
past,
Can I stand another rude and stormy blast?
Ah! the promised haven I never may attain,
Sinking and forgotten amid the lonely main;
Enemies around me, gloomy depths below—
Loose the cable, let me go!

"Lord, I would be near Thee, with Thee where
Thou art;
Thine own word hath said it, 'tis 'better to
depart.'
There to serve Thee better, there to love Thee
more,
With Thy ransomed people to worship and adore.
Ever to Thy presence Thou dost call Thine own—
Why am I remaining, helpless and alone?
Oh! to see Thy glory, Thy wondrous love to
know!
Loose the cable, let me go!

"Lord, the lights are gleaming from the distant
shore,
Where no billows threaten, where no tempests
roar.
Long-beloved voices calling me I hear—
Oh! how sweet *their* summons falls upon my ear!
Here are foes and strangers, faithless hearts and
cold;
There is fond affection, fondly proved of old!
Let me haste to join them; may it not be so?—
Loose the cable, let me go!"

Hark! the solemn answer! hark, the promise
sure!
"Blessed are the servants who to the end
endure!

Yet a little longer hope and tarry on —
Yet a little longer, weak and weary one!
More to perfect patience, to grow in faith and
  love,
More *my* strength and wisdom, and faithfulness
  to prove;
Then the sailing orders the Captain *shall* bestow—
  Loose the cable, let thee go!"

UNBEKANNTES.

Let Me Go!

LET me go! my feet are weary,
  In the desert where I roam;
Let me go! the way is dreary —
  Let the wanderer go home!
I am weary of the darkness
  Of these lonely, failing streams —
Let me go! where founts are flashing
  In the light of Heaven's beams!

Let me go! my soul is thirsting
  For those waters, bright and clear,
From the Fount of Glory bursting —
  Ah! why keep the pilgrim here?

I can catch the far-off murmurs
  Of Life's River, sweet and low,
Calling, from Earth's bitter waters,
  Unto them—Oh, let me go!

Let me go! my heart is fainting
  'Neath its weight of sins and fears,
And my wakeful eyes are failing
  With these ever-falling tears!
For the morning I am sighing,
  While I earth's long vigils keep;
Here the loved are ever dying,
  And the loving live to weep!

Let me go! I fain would follow
  Where I know their steps have passed;
Far beyond Life's heaving billows,
  Finding home and heaven at last!
While my exiled heart is pining
  To behold "my Father's" face,
They, in His own brightness shining,
  Beckon me to that blest place!

Let me go! I hear them calling,
  "Ho! thou weary one, come home!"
Words which on mine ear are falling,
  Wheresoe'er my footsteps roam.

Ah! how gladly would I listen—
  Gladly lay mine armor down,
And with eager footsteps hasten
  Where awaits the conqueror's crown!

Let me go! Oh! who would linger,
  Fainting, fearing, and athirst,
When before us lies a region
  Where undying pleasures burst?
Let me go! my soul is springing
  For its flight from Sin's dark vale,
And would fain its way be winging
  Where no storms will e'er assail!

Let me go! but, Heavenly Father!
  Thou dost hear thine orphan cry!
When around me tempests gather,
  Thou dost sit above the sky.
Trusting Thee, through Thine Anointed,
  I can yet contented roam,
Knowing, in Thine hour appointed,
  Thou wilt take the wanderer home.

A. W. B.

Not Now.

"He that had been possessed with the devil, prayed him that he might be with him."—*Mark* v. 13.

NOT *now*, my child,—a little more rough tossing—
A little longer on the billows' foam—
A few more journeyings in the desert-darkness,
And *then* the sunshine of Thy Father's Home!

Not *now*,—for I have wand'rers in the distance,
And thou must call them in with patient love;
Not *now*,—for I have sheep upon the mountains,
And thou must follow them where'er they rove.

Not *now*,—for I have loved ones sad and weary—
Wilt thou not cheer them with a kindly smile?
Sick ones, who need thee in their lonely sorrow—
Wilt thou not tend them yet a little while?

Not *now*,—for wounded hearts are sorely bleeding,
And thou must teach those widow'd hearts to sing;
Not *now*,—for orphans' tears are thickly falling—
They must be gather'd 'neath some sheltering wing.

Not *now*,—for many a hungry one is pining—
Thy willing hand must be outstretch'd and free;
Thy Father hears the mighty cry of anguish,
And gives His answering messages to thee.

Not *now*,—for dungeon walls look stern and gloomy,
And pris'ners' sighs sound strangely on the breeze—
Man's pris'ners, but thy Saviour's noble free-men—
Hast thou no ministry of love for these?

Not *now*,—for hell's eternal gulf is yawning,
And souls are perishing in hopeless sin;
Jerusalem's bright gates are standing open—
Go to the banish'd ones, and fetch them in!

Go with the name of Jesus to the dying,
And speak that Name in all its living power;
Why should thy fainting heart grow chill and weary?
Canst thou not *watch with me* one little hour?

One little hour!—and *then* the glorious crown-ing—
The golden harp-strings and the victor's palm,—
One little hour!—and *then* the Hallelujah!—
Eternity's long, deep, thanksgiving psalm!

C. P.

I'm going Home.

HEB. xi. 13.

I AM a stranger here;
No home, no rest I see;
Not all men count most dear
Can win a sigh from me —
I'm going home!

Jesus! thy home is mine,
And I, thy Father's child:
With hopes and joys divine,
The world's a weary wild —
I'm going home!

Home! oh! how soft and sweet,
It thrills upon the heart!
Home! where the brethren meet,
And never, never part—
I'm going home!

Home! where the Bridegroom takes
The purchase of his love;
Home! where the Father waits
To welcome her above —
I'm going home!

And when the world looks cold,
  Which did my Lord revile,—
A Lamb within the fold,
  I can look up and smile—
          I'm going home!

When its delusive charms
  Would snare my pilgrim feet,
I'll fly to Jesus' arms,
  And yet again repeat—
          I'm going home!

And, as the desert wide,
  The wilderness I see,
Lord Jesus! I confide
  My trembling heart to thee—
          I'm going home!

While severing every tie
  That holds me from the goal,
This, this can satisfy
  The cravings of the soul—
          I'm going home!

Ah! gently, *gently* lead
  Along the painful way;
Bid every word and deed,
  And every look to say—
          I'm going home!

My Father.

"'IS this the way, my Father?'—''Tis, my child;
Thou must pass through the tangled, dreary wild,
If thou wouldst reach the city undefiled,—
Thy peaceful home above.'

"'But enemies are round?'—'Yes, child, I know
That where thou least expect'st thou'lt find a foe;
But victor thou shalt prove o'er all below,—
Only, seek strength above.'

"'My Father, it is dark.'—'Child, take my hand;
Cling close to me,—I'll lead thee through the land;
Trust my all-seeing care,—so shalt thou stand
Midst glory bright above.'

"'My footsteps seem to slide.'—'Child, only raise
Thine eye to me, then in these slippery ways,
I will hold up thy goings; thou shalt praise
Me for each step above.'

"'O Father, I'm weary!'—'Child, lean thy head
Upon my breast; it was my love that spread
Thy rugged path; hope on still, till I have said,
'Rest,—rest for aye above.'"

J. B. M.

The Fulness of Jesus.

"WHY should I fear the darkest hour,
Or tremble at the tempest's power?
Jesus vouchsafes to be my *Tower!*

"Though hot the fight, why quit the field?
Why must I either flee or yield,
Since Jesus is my mighty *Shield?*

"When creature comforts fade and die,
Worldlings may weep, but why should I?
Jesus still lives, and still is *nigh!*

"I know not what may soon betide,
Nor how my wants may be supplied;
But Jesus knows, and '*will provide.*'

"Though sin would fill me with distress,
The throne of grace I dare address;
For Jesus is my *Righteousness.*

"Though faint my prayers, and cold my love,
My steadfast hope shall not remove,
While Jesus *intercedes* above.

"Against me earth and hell combine,
But on my side is power Divine:
Jesus is *all*, and He is *mine.*"

"Come Away."

"THE leaves around me falling,
Are preaching of decay;
The hollow winds are calling,
'Come, pilgrim, come away!'
The day, in night declining,
Says, 'I must too decline;'
The year, its life resigning,
Its lot foreshadows mine.

"The light my path surrounding,
The loves to which I cling,
The hopes within me bounding,
The joys that round me wing;
All melt, like stars of even,
Before the morning's ray,
Pass upwards into heaven,
And chide at my delay.

"The friends gone there before me
Are calling from on high,
And joyous angels o'er me
Tempt sweetly to the sky.
'Why wait,' they say, 'and wither,
'Mid scenes of death and sin?
Oh! rise to glory hither,
And find true life begin.'

"I hear the invitation,
And fain would rise and come,
A sinner to salvation,
An exile to his home.
But while I here must linger,
Thus, thus, let all I see
Point on, with faithful finger,
To heaven, O Lord! and Thee."

H. F. LYTE.

The Yearning Spirit.

"WHY thus longing, thus for ever sighing,
For the far off, unattain'd and dim,
While the beautiful, all round thee lying,
Offers up its low, perpetual hymn?

"Wouldst thou listen to its gentle teaching,
All the restless yearnings it would still;
Leaf and flower, and laden bee, are preaching,
Thine own sphere, though humble, first to fill.

"Poor indeed thou must be, if around thee
Thou no ray of light and joy canst throw;
If no silken cord of love hath bound thee
To some little world through weal and woe:

"If no dear eyes thy fond love can brighten,
No fond voices answer to thine own;
If no brother's sorrow thou canst lighten,
By daily sympathy and gentle tone.

"Not by deeds that the crowd applauses,
Not by works that give the world renown,
Not by martyrdom, or vaunted crosses,
Canst thou win and wear the immortal crown.

"Daily struggling, though enclosed and lonely,
Every day a rich reward will give;
Thou wilt find, by hearty striving only,
And truly loving, thou canst truly live."

"Thou wilt not Forget Me."

"AND wilt Thou now forget me, Lord?
Oh, no! it cannot be;
No earthly tongue can ever tell
What Thou hast been to me.

"Through all the chequer'd scenes of life
Thy love hath shelter'd me;
And wilt Thou now forsake Thy child?
Oh, no! it cannot be.

"In life, or death, I take my stand,
Where I have ever stood,
Beneath the shelter of Thy cross,
And trusting in Thy blood.

"And there, when youth, and health, and strength,
And energy have fled,
The shades of evening, peacefully,
Shall close around my head."

Heavenly Home.

"LET me go! let me go! for the is day breaking,
The skies have a streak of orient light;
The shadow of darkness the earth is forsaking,
And the sunbeams are chasing the mists of the night!

"Let me go! let me go! for I may not tarry;
Hinder me not, for my home is there,
Where angels are waiting my spirit to carry,
And the pure, white raiment is ready to wear!

"Let me go! let me go! for the purple dawning,
Is mantling the dull, dark tomb of Time;
And there stealeth the rays of a blissful morning
That blushes and burns in a deathless clime!

" I have done with sin, I have done with sorrow;
 I fly to the spotless realms of light,
Where the day that is breaking shall have no morrow,
 And the sun that is rising, shall have no night!"

Heart Hymn.

BEAR the burden of the present,
 Let the morrow bear its own;
If the morning sky be pleasant,
 Why the coming night bemoan?

If the darkened heavens lower,
 Wrap thy cloak around thy form;
Though the tempest rise in power,
 God is mightier than the storm.

Steadfast faith, and hope unshaken,
 Animate the trusting breast;
Step by step the journey's taken
 Nearer to the land of rest.

All unseen, the Master walketh
 By the toiling servant's side;
Comfortable words He talketh,
 While His hands uphold and guide.

Grief, nor pain, nor any sorrow,
  Rends thy breast, to Him unknown;
He to-day, and He to-morrow,
  Grace sufficient gives His own.

Holy strivings nerve and strengthen—
  Long endurance wins the crown;
When the evening shadows lengthen,
  Thou shalt lay the burden down.

Easter Hymn.

"The Lord is risen! He is risen indeed!"—Thus saluted and responded the early Christians.

JOY! Thou art risen! Never mortal anguish
    Shall press Thee now!
Never again beneath the cross Thou'lt languish,
    And fainting, bow!

Joy! that throughout eternity's duration
    Thou canst not know
Again the desert's dark humiliation—
    Gethsemane's wo!

Joy! that forever from thy heart is taken
    The cursed load
That broke it in the cry, "I am forsaken!
    My God! my God!"

Risen!—to all dominion, power, and glory!
My humbled soul
Bows in adoring reverence before Thee—
Owns thy control.

In joyful song of love and of thanksgiving,
My voice I lift.
Because Thou livest, I am also living—
My life, Thy gift.

For me no wo of Thine be vainly wasted!
I may not rest
In pleasant sweets—the bitter cup untasted—
Thy dear lips pressed.

A baptism, deep unto my childish stature,
With Thee I share:
A cross, made heavy by my feeble nature
For Thee I bear.

Only those words of utter desolation,—
Thine, Thine alone,—
Even in hours of deepest tribulation,
I may not own.

* * * * * *

Risen with Thee, dear Lord! and dare I name it!
From death-bonds freed!
Let every step of my new life proclaim it—
"Risen indeed!"

The Christian and his Echo.

TRUE faith, producing love to God and man,
Say, Echo, is not this the Gospel plan?
The Gospel plan.

Must I my faith and love to Jesus show
By doing good to all, both friend and foe?
Both friend and foe.

But if a brother hates and treats me ill,
Must I return him good, and love him still?
Love him still.

If he my failings watches to reveal,
Must I his faults as carefully conceal?
As carefully conceal.

But if my name and character he blast,
And cruel malice, too, a long time last;
And if I sorrow and affliction know
He loves to add unto my cup of woe;
In this uncommon, this peculiar case,
Sweet Echo, say, must I still love and bless?
Still love and bless.

Whatever usage ill I may receive,
Must I be patient still, and still forgive?
Be patient still, and still forgive.

Why, Echo, how is this? thou'rt sure a dove!
Thy voice shall teach me nothing else but love!
Nothing else but love.

Amen! with all my heart, then be it so;
'Tis all delightful, just, and good, I know:
And now to practise I'll directly go.
Directly go.

Things being so, whoever me reject,
My gracious God me surely will protect.
Surely will protect.

Henceforth I'll roll on him my every care,
And then both friend and foe embrace in prayer.
Embrace in prayer.

But after all those duties I have done,
Must I, in point of merit, them disown,
And trust for heaven through Jesus' blood alone?
Through Jesus' blood alone.

Echo, enough! thy counsels to mine ear,
Are sweeter than, to flowers, the dew-drop tear;
Thy wise instructive lessons please me well:
I'll go and practise them. Farewell, farewell.
PRACTISE them. Farewell, farewell.

The Father's Rod.

EZEKIEL XX. 37.

I SAW the young bride in her beauty and pride,
Bedeck'd in her snowy array;
And the bright flash of joy mantled high on her cheek,
And the future look'd blooming and gay.

With woman's devotion she laid her fond heart
On the shrine of idolatrous love:
She anchor'd her hopes to this perishing earth,
By the chain which her tenderness wove.

But I saw, when those heart-strings were bleeding and torn,
And the chain had been sever'd in two,
She had changed her white robes for the sables of grief,
And her bloom for the paleness of woe.

But the Healer was there pouring balm on her heart,
And wiping the tears from her eyes;
And He strengthen'd the chain He had sever'd in twain,
And fasten'd it firm to the skies.

There had whisper'd a voice—
'Twas the voice of her God,
"I love thee, I love thee,
Pass under the rod."

I saw a young mother in tenderness bend
O'er the couch of her slumbering boy:
And she kiss'd the soft lips as they murmur'd her
name,
As the sleeper lay dreaming in joy.

Oh! sweet as the rose-bud encircled with dew,
When its fragrance is flung on the air,
So fresh and so bright to the mother he seem'd,
As he lay in his innocence there..

But I saw when she gazed on the same lovely
form,
Pale as marble, and silent, and cold;
But paler and colder her beautiful boy—
And the tale of her sorrow was told.

But the Healer was there, who had smitten her
heart,
And taken her treasure away:
To allure *her* to heaven, He had placed *it* on high,
And the mourner will sweetly obey.

There had whisper'd a voice—
'Twas the voice of her God,
"I love thee, I love thee,
Pass under the rod."

I saw when a father and mother had leaned
On the arms of a dear cherish'd son;
And the star in the future grew bright to their gaze,
As they saw the proud place he had won.

And the fast coming evening of life promised fair,
And the pathway grew smooth to their feet,
And the star-light of love glimmer'd bright at the end,
And the whispers of fancy were sweet.

But I saw when they stood, bending low o'er the grave,
Where their heart's dearest hope had been laid,
And the star had gone down in the darkness of night,
And joy from their bosoms had fled.

But the Healer was there, and His arms were around,
And He led them with tenderest care;
And He show'd them a star in the bright upper world:
'Twas *their* star shining brilliantly there.

They had each heard a voice—
'Twas the voice of their God,
"I love thee, I love thee,
Pass under the rod."

Lines on "My Father's Bible."

FRIEND of my earliest childhood's opening days!
What tides of feeling swell within my soul
As on thy well-worn russet garb I gaze,
And busy memory's backward currents roll.

How oft, with living power thy hallowed word,
Borne on a Father's voice has sought mine ear,
Whilst God's own Spirit in my bosom stirred,
And whispering, taught me, "'Tis Thy Life to hear."

How oft a sainted mother's gentle hand
Has led my youthful eye to search thy page,
Whilst she would fondly urge her blest command
To make Thee guide in youth, and hope in age.

How often from thy precepts have I turned,
Whilst with the law's convincing power I strove;
What fires of joy within my soul have burned,
Caught from thy record of a Saviour's love.

Guide of my father's path — my mother's stay —
Be thou my comfort on life's thorny road, —
Lead me with them to seek that blessed "way" —
Through whom alone they sought Heaven's bright abode.

My father's Bible! Oh, my father's God, —
Thanks for a father that hath loved thy law!
Teach me to heed the path that he hath trod,
And living waters from thy fountains draw.

Thanks for a mother passed into the skies,
Treasured among the *jewels* of thy love!
Give me on wings of faith like her to rise,
And seek my home in that blest world above.

DR. C. P. M.

Philadelphia, 1864.

Sickness Sanctified.

HE came, the sweet angel my Father assigned,
  To watch o'er my path to the sky;
I knew not if yet from that path I'd declined,
  Or if only temptation was nigh.
He touched me: the body shrank back from his
    touch,
  But my spirit with ecstacy glowed;
It longed to be free, for its prospects were such
  As no pains of the body could cloud.

My Father! I deemed thou hadst called me to
    dwell
  In the rest thou'st prepared above;
But I find myself still in the flesh — it is well;
  If I go, if I stay, it is love.
Love ordered the plan; and, in love such as thine,
  How shall I not calmly confide!
Who spared not, to save me, a ransom divine,
  The Lamb who on Calvary died.

Oh, welcome the sufferings, whenever they come,
  That bring with them comforts like these;
Let me always be filled with such foretastes of
    home,
  And I sigh not for health and for ease.

That angel's soft touch thus again would I feel,
Though my heartstrings with agony quiver,
The pressure is mercy, it wounds but to heal,
It will end in enjoyment forever.

Oh! when shall I shake off these trammels of flesh,
And reach that eternal abode?
Where the joys I so value shall blossom afresh,
Revived by the smiles of my God.
Shall I think the embrace that dissolves them too cold?
Shall I think the short journey too drear?
When the arms of a Saviour my spirit enfold,
And the gates of the city appear?

No: welcome the summons that bids me depart,
And welcome that moment to me,
When the clog from my spirit death strikes with his dart,
And bids it forever be free.
Lord Jesus! I then in thy glory shall share,
And forever be blest with thy sight;
Then all will be tranquil, and all will be fair,
And all will be endless delight.

The Crown of Stars.

"They that be wise shall shine as the brightness of the firmament; and they that turn many to righteousness, as the stars for ever and ever."—DAN. xii. 3.

"Let them crown themselves with rose-buds, but crown thou me with twelve stars."—AN OLD WRITER.

THE rose-bud hangs upon the thorn,
(No flower on earth so fair),
Go choose thee, on a summer morn,
The crown that thou wilt wear.

But ere the eventide is nigh,
The evening chill and gray,
When stars are set in yonder sky,
The flowers will droop away.

The clinging thorn thy wreath will be,
(It pierces deep, I know;)
Go choose that changing crown for thee,
But I will crownless go.

There was a cold and bitter dawn,
(Long ages since have fled;)
From gloomy brakes men snatched the thorn
To crown my Master's head.

The sinless brow grew deathly pale,
  The blood fell heavily:
Think ye the rose-wreath, fair and frail,
  A fitting crown for me?

Nay, crownless I will wend my way,
  Though yonder rose is sweet,
Until, on earth's wild gath'ring day,
  My thorn-crowned King I meet.

Then, if my Saviour owneth me,
  Accepted in his sight,
The stars of heaven my crown shall be,
  That will not fade at night.

The rose-bud hangs upon the thorn—
  No flower on earth so fair—
But I have hope, that endless morn,
  A crown of stars to wear.

Consolation.

The following original poem is by the lamented CHARLOTTE ELIZABETH.

WHEN the streamlet is dried up,
  Then fly to the fountain;
When the valley is flooded,
  Then haste to the mountain:
When the arm thou hast leant on
  Is laid in the dust,
On the arm of thy God
  Lean with faith's cheerful trust.

Earth's gourds! Oh, how tempting
  Their flowers and their fruit!
How we love their sweet shadow!—
  A worm's at the root!
Is thy gourd that once sheltered,
  Now withered away?
Be the shadow of Jesus
  Thy shelter and stay!

How oft have hope's visions
  Deceived the fond-hearted!
Like the rainbow they shone,
  Like the rainbow departed:

When the light that once sparkled
  Is darkened and gone,
See! the rainbow that fades not,
  It arches God's throne!

How oft have earth's pleasures,
  For which our hearts panted,
Like the bright poison-berry,
  Proved deadly when granted!
When the soul has been sickened
  With earth's poisoned joy,
Look up for true pleasures,—
  Their fountain's on high!

As the dove, when of old,
  From the ark it went forth,
Some green spot to rest on,
  To seek through the earth;
When it found that the deluge,
  So deep and so dark,
Left no green spot uncovered,
  Returned to the ark—

So, when floods of affliction
  Have deluged all round,
And no green spot of gladness,
  No hope-branch is found,

Then flee to the Saviour,
 The true ark of rest!
Oh! there's no place of shelter
 Like his pitying breast.

When there thou art sheltered,
 Though storms wrap the skies,
And higher and higher
 The deep floods arise, —
Above the dark waters
 The ark's lifted high,
And bears its best inmates
 To God's mount, the sky.

By the scorn and the scoffing,
 For thy sake he bore;
By the sharp crown of thorns,
 For thy sake he wore;
By the sweat in the garden,
 The death on the tree, —
To him who redeemed thee,
 Thou wearied one, flee.

From him, thine own Saviour,
 Whate'er may betide thee,
No sorrow can sever,
 No distance divide thee.

Earth's friends *may* forsake,
  But he'll forsake never;
Earth's loved ones *must die*,
  But he lives *for ever!*

In love he afflicts thee,
  In mercy he chastens;
To wound he is slow,
  But to bind up he hastens;
When thy sins call for chast'ning,
  'Twill comfort impart,
Though a frown's on his brow,
  Yet there's love in his heart!

Each dear earthly cistern
  By his hand may be broken;
But the stroke, though severe,
  Of his love is a token.
He breaks them, that we
  By their loss may be led
To drink of pure pleasures
  From joy's fountain-head.

To him, who so loved thee,
  Let grief draw thee nearer;
Each dear, precious promise,
  Let sorrow make dearer:

And welcome the trial,
  By which there is given
To thy soul more of God,
  To thy heart more of heaven!

"He Restoreth my Soul."

PSALM xxiii.

COLD on the mountain brow,
  A wandering lambkin lay;
No fold receives it now,
  Though near the close of day:
Ill can it brook the mountain air,
Nor grass, nor water finds it there.

It knew not it was weak—
  Forgot the foes around;
Its pleasures it would seek
  Upon forbidden ground;—
Despised its Shepherd's voice; and now
Must die upon the mountain brow.

And is there none to save?
  And must the wanderer die?
Around its mountain grave
  It casts a fearful eye:
And hears—and how does it rejoice
To hear again the Shepherd's voice.

Braving the mountain air—
  Braving the wintry wind:
Who would such perils dare
  A wandering lamb to find?
All its ingratitude forgot,
He owns as it had wandered not!

Pressed to his bosom dear,
  Securely to repose:
This lamb has learned to fear,
  And all its weakness knows:
Has learnt to trust its gentle guide,
And find its safety by his side.

Unfit to fight or fly,
  Though compassed round with foes,
That foolish lamb am I,
  My heart the picture knows:
Yet fears not, shrinks not, from the view,
For I've a tender Shepherd too.

How often have I stayed!
 How often has he sought,
And all my tears assuaged!
 And shall not I be taught
Like it to tremble at my foes,
And on his love find sweet repose?

And did the lamb rejoice
 When ransomed from the grave?
O! let me raise my voice
 To him who died to save!
What is the lamb compared to me?
Its shepherd what, my Lord, to thee?

E. S. A.

Earth's Sunny Spots.

WHAT though we wander in a maze,
 Bestrewed with many a thorn!
What though across the stream of time
 Our bark be rudely borne!
What though we number weary hours,
 When life appears a blot!
Still may we find, to cheer our hearts,
 There's many a sunny spot.

Though on the present, with its cares,
  No light is seen to fall,
And o'er the page of future years
  Despair has spread her pall;
Yet early days of childhood's mirth,
  What heart remembers not,
When hope's bright dreams made all so fair,
  Earth seemed one sunny spot.

The heedless foot may press the flowers,
  And odors from them bring;
Thus, oft in sorrow's deepest night
  Faith's sweetest blossoms spring.
If thou hast dried the widow's tear,
  Pitied the orphan's lot,
Then hast thou *felt*, amid the gloom,
  There was a sunny spot.

If to the humble couch of pain,
  Aid thou hast kindly brought,
And poured upon a wounded heart
  The balm it vainly sought;
If thou in prayer hast meekly bent
  Within the lowly cot,
Then *thou* hast in life's desert proved
  Thyself a sunny spot.

Then, what though down the stream of time
  Thy bark be rudely driven,
Thy pilot's hand is ever near,
  To guide thee safe to heaven.
Earth's weary children then shall find—
  When, every care forgot,
They calmly rest secure from fears—
  Their heaven a sunny spot.

Light in the Darkness.

THE earth grew dark, and darker yet
  Than the mid-watch of night,
Her stars were lost, her sun was set,
  The nations wept for light.

Bright angel faces, now and then,
  Looked from the clouded skies,
And some among the sons of men
  Beheld their beaming eyes.

But evil spirits trod the earth,
  Whom none had strength to bind;
The tones of their unholy mirth
  Rose on the moaning wind.

Watchers from many a mountain hold
  Were looking earnestly,
And saw no streak of morning gold
  Afar o'er land or sea.

That hour, the holy face of one,
  Brighter than earthly day,
Gazed through the gloom, and saw that none
  Would rend the veil away.

His robes of majesty he tore,
  Clothed as a servant then,
A lamp of wondrous power he bore
  Through many a sunless den.

And some beheld the holy brow
  With earth's thick mantle veiled,
As men behold the morning now,
  The light of lights they hailed.

They saw him 'neath the eastern skies —
  The memory stirs us yet;
Our faith looks back with eager eyes
  Earth will no more forget.

Said I, we would forget no more —
  What means the thoughtless brow
That passes many a temple door,
  Where Christ is present now?

Said I, we would forget no more —
What means it that we tread
Smiling, where Jesus wept of yore
Amongst the living dead?

Said I, we would forget no more —
Alas! thou feeble heart,
Hast thou not suffered o'er and o'er
The memory to depart?

Violets.

"Love, and compassion, and meekness. . . These violets grow low, and are of a dark color, yet they are of a very sweet and diffusive smell."—Archbishop Leighton.

SO spake a pilgrim, on his way
Through fading earthly bowers,
Whose cruse of waters, day by day,
Nurtured these lovely flowers;

Flowers that in tangled thickets grow,
Half lost the leaves beneath,
While oftentimes the cold white snow
Drops on their purple wreath.

Their simple urn is lifted up
  Day after day, to heaven,
And often to the sapphire cup
  The early rain is given.

Love, pity, meekness—these are they—
  The violets, dim and wild,
Clust'ring in many a woodland way,
  Before the cottage child.

They sprang beside a lowly door,
  In Galilee of old,
And now upon our northern shore
  They shudder with the cold.

They tremble sorely, but they live
  In shadowed nooks, and lone;
The pleasant fragrance that they give
  Across the seas hath gone.

A child may tend these woodland flowers
  Who could not nurse the rose;
May watch, through bleak and sunless hours,
  Their simple buds unclose.

Oh! quiet blossoms, wild and dark,
  How thickly set they spring
Amongst earth's tangled thorns, to mark
  The foot-prints of our King!

And for the sake of him who sowed,
  We love their clusters sweet,
And sorrow when their stalks are bowed
  By rude and worldly feet.

On the cold earth they shall not die;
  Plucked from the burial mound,
Their roots, by angels borne on high,
  Shall bloom in holier ground.

Charity.

I SEE, beneath a wintry sky,
  A boy go forth to sow;
By earnest eyes, and quiet step,
  He must be Faith, I know.

I see a smiling child look up
  The parted cloud between;
She smiles as none but Hope can smile,
  For heaven is dimly seen.

I see another, meek of brow,
  Lift up a wounded bee,
That lately stung her loving hand,
  And she is Charity.

Faith ploughs and sows this evil earth,
Hope watches changeful skies,
But Charity shall dwell in heaven,
With bright and tearless eyes.

Easter Thoughts.

HOW dark, and how narrow, how thronged is the home,
Where the feet of the weary ones noiselessly come!
The poor and the mighty its threshold have trod,
And the footprints of children are deep in the sod.

That threshold was darker in ages gone by,
Ere the star of the holy arose in the sky;
The tears of the elders were bitterly shed
When they opened that door to the pale-shrouded dead.

Of all the bright sunbeams their summers had known,
Not one golden arrow had broken the stone—
The stone that was lying, so hard and so cold,
At the doors of the sleepers, the weak and the bold.

There came a fair morning (long ages are past),
And the death-fettered nations were loosened at last;
The hand of the Mighty broke open the door,
And the feet of his people are holden no more.

Like reeds by a river the mourners were bow'd,
When they folded at even the Christ in his shroud:
But light in the darkness, and joy in the grave,
Have been known since he entered, the Mighty, to save.

The night has departed, the morning is now,
And there hovers a glory half-seen on the brow—
That bears in its last pallid slumber the cross,
And hath borne it through sorrow, through shame, and through loss.

O! bright Easter morning, that tarries awhile,
And yet surely on earth and her kingdoms shall smile,—
When life from the fount to our lips shall be given,
And the blessed shall shine as the stars in the heaven.

This hope is your glory, true servants of God,
In its light the dark valley of death will be trod,
And see ye the little ones, thronging the land,
With their torches unkindled, and Easter at hand!

Oh, rise ye up early at the dawn of the day,
And behold where your Lord in the sepulchre
lay!
The soul will be willing, the tongue will be bold,
And in cities and hamlets the news will be told.

"The Little While."

OH, for the peace that floweth like a river,
Making life's desert places bloom and smile!
Oh, for the faith to grasp Heaven's bright "for-
ever,"
Amid the shadow of earth's "little while!"

"A little while" for patient vigil keeping,
To face the stern, to wrestle with the strong.
"A little while" to sow the seed with weeping,
Then bind the sheaves and sing the harvest
song!

"A little while" to wear the robe of sadness,
To toil with weary step through miry ways,
Then to pour forth the fragrant robe of gladness,
And clasp the girdle round the robe of praise!

"A little while," 'midst shadow and illusion
To strive, by faith, love's mysteries to spell;
Then read each dark enigma's bright solution,
Whilst meekly owning, "He doeth all things well."

"A little while" the earthen pitcher taking
To wayside brooks, from far-off fountains fed,
When the cool lip its thirst forever slaking,
May taste the fulness of the Fountain Head!

"A little while" to keep the oil from failing,—
"A little while" faith's flickering lamp to trim;
And then the Bridegroom's coming footsteps hailing,
To haste to meet him with the bridal hymn.

And he who is himself the Gift and Giver,
The future glory, and the present smile,
With the bright promise of the glad "forever"
Will light the shadows of the "little while."

J. C.

Leave the Future with God.

THOU, whose sad and darkling brow,
Seems to tell of care and woe,
Dost thou pour upon the cloud
That futurity doth shroud?
And thy trembling fancy fill
With anticipated ill?
Ask these flowrets of the field
For the lessons they can yield.
Hark! to fancy's listening ear,
Thus they whisper, soft and clear:
Heaven-appointed teachers we,
Mortal! we would counsel thee;
Gratefully enjoy to-day,
If the sun vouchsafe his ray,
If the darkling tempest lower,
Meekly bend beneath the shower;
But, oh! leave to-morrow's fare
To thy heavenly Father's care.
Does each day upon its wing
Its allotted burden bring?
Load it not besides with sorrow,
Which belongeth to the morrow.

Strength is promised, strength is given,
When the heart by God is riven;
But foredate the day of woe,
And, *alone*, thou bear'st the blow!
One thing only claims thy care, —
Seek thou first, by faith and prayer,
That all-glorious world above,
Scene of righteousness and love;
And, whate'er thou need'st below,
He thou trustest will bestow.

ANON.

Gethsemane.

JESUS, while he dwelt below,
  As divine historians say,
To a place would often go;
  Near to Kedron's brook it lay;
In this place he loved to be;
And 'twas named Gethsemane.

'Twas a garden, as we read,
  At the foot of Olivet, —
Low, and proper to be made
  The Redeemer's lone retreat;
When from noise he would be free,
Then he sought Gethsemane.

Thither by their Master brought,
  His disciples likewise came;
There the heavenly truths he taught
  Often set their hearts on flame;
Therefore they, as well as he,
Visited Gethsemane.

Oft conversing here they sat,
  Or might join with Christ in prayer;
Oh! what blest devotion's that,
  When the Lord himself is there!
All things to them seem'd to agree
To endear Gethsemane.

Full of love to man's lost race,
  On the conflict much he thought;
This he knew the destined place,
  And he loved the sacred spot;
Therefore Jesus chose to be
Often in Gethsemane.

Came at length the dreadful night;
  Vengeance, with its iron rod,
Stood, and, with collected might,
  Bruised the harmless Lamb of God.
See, my soul, thy Saviour see,
Prostrate in Gethsemane!

View him in that olive press,
  Wrung with anguish, whelm'd in blood!
Hear him pray in his distress,
  With strong cries and tears, to God;
Then reflect, what sin must be,
Gazing on Gethsemane.

Gloomy garden, on thy beds,
  Washed by Kedron's water-pool,
Grow most rank and bitter weeds;
  Think on these, my soul, my soul!
Wouldst thou sin's dominion see?
Call to mind Gethsemane.

Eden, from each flowery bed,
  Did for man short sweetness breathe;
Soon, by Satan's counsel led,
  Man wrought sin, and sin wrought death;
But of life, the healing tree
Grows in rich Gethsemane.

Hither, Lord, thou didst resort
  Oftimes with thy little train;
Here wouldst keep thy private court,
  Oh! confer that grace again:
Lord, resort with worthless me
Oft-times to Gethsemane.

True, I can't deserve to share
  In a favor so divine;
But, since sin first fixed thee there,
  None have greater sins than mine;
And to this, my woeful plea,
Witness thou, Gethsemane!

Sins against a holy God;
  Sins against his righteous laws;
Sins against his love, his blood;
  Sins against his name and cause;
Sins immense as is the sea;
Hide me, O Gethsemane!

Saviour, all the stone remove
  From my flinty, frozen heart;
Thaw it with the beams of love,
  Pierce it with thy mercy's dart;
Wound the heart that wounded thee;
Break it in Gethsemane!

"Fear Not."

"Fear not. . . . . . I have the keys of the grave and of death."

OH, cling not, trembler, to life's fragile bark;
It fills — it soon must sink.
Look not below, where all is chill and dark;
'Tis agony to think
Of that wild waste; but look, oh! look above,
And see the outstretched arm of Love.

Cling not to this poor life; unlock thy clasp
Of fleeting, vapory air.
The world receding soon will mock thy grasp;
But let the wings of prayer
Take the blest breeze of heaven, and upward flee,
And life from God shall enter thee.

Oh, fear not him who walks the stormy wave;
'Tis not a spectre, but the Lord.
Trust thou in him who overcame the grave,
Who holds in captive ward
The powers of hell. Heed not the monster grim,
Nor fear to go through death to him.

Look not so fondly back on this false earth;
  Let hope not linger here.
Say, would the worm forego its second birth,
  Or the transition fear,
That gives it wings to try a world unknown,
Although it wakes and mounts alone?

But thou art not alone; on either side
  The portal, friends stand guard,
And the kind spirits wait thy course to guide.
  Why, why should it be hard,
To trust our Maker with the soul he gave,
Or him who died that soul to save?

Into his hands commit thy trembling spirit,
  Who gave his life for thine.
Guilty, fix all thy trust upon His merit;
  To him thy heart resign.
Oh, give him love for love, and sweetly fall
Into his hands, who is thy all.

CONDER.

"The World to be Crucified."

"By whom the world is crucified to me, and I unto the world."

NEVER further than thy cross!
Never higher than thy feet!
Here earth's precious things seem dross,
Here earth's bitter things seems sweet.

Gazing thus, our sin we see;
Learn thy love while gazing thus;
Sin, which laid the cross on thee;
Love, which bore the cross for us.

Here from pomp and pride retired,
Nothing we would seem to be;
Dust, yet with thy life inspired;
Nothing, yet beloved by thee.

Symbols of our liberty,
And our service here unite;
Captives, by thy cross made free;
Soldiers of thy cross, we fight.

Pressing onward as we can,
  Still to this our life shall tend;
Where life's earliest steps began,
  May life's latest moments end.

Till, amid the hosts of light,
  We, in the redeemed, complete,
Through thy cross made pure and bright,
  Cast our crowns before thy feet.

Peace in Trouble.

AMONG the wonders of God's power
  Is that it can give us peace,
While the dreaded blow descends,
  While the joys we cherished, cease.

'Tis not that the stroke is light,
  Or that we should count it small,
But the grace that with it comes
  Sanctifies and sweetens all.

Yet this blessing is reserved
  Only for the smitten heart;
He alone the balm may taste
  Who hath felt the bitter smart.

Thou may'st less of sorrow know,
  It may be high heaped o'er me,
But a feast for me is spread
  That was never spread for thee.

Not that I am thus upheld
  While thy steps are left to slide;
Mine are heavier weights of grief,
  Mine are fuller joys beside.

Why should I from trouble shrink,
  Or new woes refuse to bear,
If they are Christ's messengers,
  Charged with blessings rich and rare?

Not beneath unclouded skies,
  Not midst smooth prosperity,
Doth it please our risen Lord
  We his form, most plain, should see;

But when storm and tempest blow,
  Then he calls us by our name;
While beneath us rolls the flood,
  While around us roars the flame!

The Starless Crown.

"They that turn many to righteousness shall shine as the stars for ever and ever."—DANIEL xii. 3.

WEARIED and worn with earthly cares, I yielded to repose,
And, soon before my raptured sight, a glorious vision rose:
I thought, whilst slumbering on my couch, in midnight's solemn gloom,
I heard an angel's silvery voice, and radiance filled my room.
A gentle touch awaken'd me,—a gentle whisper said,
"Arise, O sleeper, follow me;" and through the air we fled:
We left the earth, so far away that like a speck it seem'd,
And heavenly glory, calm and pure, across our pathway stream'd.
Still on we went,—my soul was wrapped in silent ecstacy;
I wondered what the end would be, what next should meet mine eye.

I knew not how we journeyed through the pathless fields of light,
When suddenly a change was wrought, and *I was clothed in white.*
We stood before a city's walls most glorious to behold;
We passed through gates of glistening pearl, o'er streets of purest gold;
It needed not the sun by day, the silver moon by night;
The glory of the Lord was there, the Lamb himself its light.
Bright angels paced the shining streets, sweet music filled the air,
And white-robed saints with glittering crowns, from every clime were there;
And some that I had loved on earth stood with them round the throne.
"All worthy is the Lamb," they sang, "the glory his alone."
But fairer far than all beside, I saw my Saviour's face;
And as I gazed he smiled on me with wondrous love and grace.
Lowly I bowed before his throne, o'erjoyed that I at last
Had gained the object of my hopes; that earth at length was past.

And then in solemn tones he said, "Where is the diadem
That ought to sparkle on thy brow—adorned with many a gem?
I know thou hast believed on me, and life through me is thine,
But where are all those radiant stars that in thy crown should shine?
Yonder thou seest a glorious throng, and stars on every brow!
For every soul they led to me they wear a jewel now!
And such *thy* bright reward had been if such had been thy *deed*,
If thou hadst sought some wand'ring feet in path of peace to lead.
I did not mean that thou should'st tread the way of life *alone*,
But that the clear and shining light which round thy footsteps shone,
Should guide some other weary feet to my bright home of rest,
And thus, in blessing those around, thou hadst thyself been blest."

*　　*　　*　　*　　*　　*

The vision faded from my sight, the voice no longer spake,
A spell seemed brooding o'er my soul which long I feared to break,

And when at last I gazed around in morning's
glimmering light,
My spirit fell o'erwhelmed beneath that vision's
awful might.
I rose and wept with chastened joy that yet I
dwelt below,
That yet another hour was mine my faith by
works to show;
That yet some sinner I might tell of Jesus' dying
love,
And help to lead some weary soul to seek a home
above.
And now, while on the earth I stay, my motto
this shall be,
"To live no longer to myself, but him who died
for me!"
And graven on my inmost soul this word of truth
divine,
"*They that turn many to the Lord, bright as the
stars shall shine.*"

S. S. TREASURY.

Sabbath Longings.

NOW in this holy hour,
When cares of earth no more my bosom press,
Wilt thou, O, Highest, give my spirit power
To catch some glimpses of the land of rest,
And taste the joys reserved for all the blest!

Awake, my inmost soul!
Mount upward to those blessed regions fair,
Beyond the influence of earth's control,
Where sin and pain, and want, and woe, and care,
'Mid heaven's entrancing joys forgotten are.

Rest on the flowery plain,
Where the Good Shepherd feeds his flock so dear;
And list the melody of that sweet strain
With which he softly charms the enraptured ear
Of all his tender lambs reposing near.

Oh! of that beauteous tree,
(Which on the brink of life's bright river grows,
And yields its blessed fruit perennially),
Partake with joy, and of the stream which flows
Through heaven's green meadows,—drink, and heal thy woes.

O High and Holy Power!
Creation's soul, that giveth life and light
To high archangel, as to tiny flower,
Oh, that *my* soul to thee united quite,
Might soar away to everlasting light.

Nearer to Life's Winter.

NEARER to life's winter, wife,
We are drawing nearer,
Memories of our blessed spring
Growing dearer, dearer.

Through the summer heats we've toiled,
Through the autumn weather,
We have almost passed, sweet wife,
Hand-in-hand together.

Time was, hearts were, well as feet,
Lighter, I remember;
April's locks of gold are turned
Silver this November.

Flowers are fewer than at first,
  And the way grows drearer,
For unto life's winter, wife,
  We are drawing nearer.

Nearer to life's end, sweet wife,
  We are drawing nearer;
The last mile-stone on the way,
  To our sight grows clearer.

Some whose hands we held grew faint,
  And lay down to slumber;
Looking backward, we to-day
  All their graves may number.

Heights we've sought we've failed to climb,
  Fruits we've failed to gather;
But what matter, since we've still
  Jesus and each other?

"Mighty to Save."

From the pen of a dear departed youth, who lately fell asleep in Jesus, in his sixteenth year. The lines were, with many others, found in his pocket-book after his departure.

OH! I have been at the brink of the grave,
And stood on the edge of its deep, dark wave;
And I thought in the still, calm hours of night,
Of those regions where all is ever bright;
And I feared not the wave
Of the gloomy grave,
For I knew that Jehovah was "mighty to save."

I have watched the solemn ebb and flow
Of life's tide, which was fleeting sure, tho' slow;
I've stood on the shore of Eternity,
And heard the deep roar of its rushing sea;
Yet I feared not the wave
Of the gloomy grave.
For I knew that Jehovah was "mighty to save."

And I found that my only rest could be
In the death of the One who died for me;
For my rest is bought with the price of blood,
Which gushed from the veins of the Son of God:
So I fear not the wave
Of the gloomy grave,
For I know that Jehovah is "mighty to save."

L. T.

BANKS OF THE CLWYD, May 6, 1858.

The Divine Response.

IN the darkness will I prove thee,
Hide the love wherewith I love thee,
Lead thee with an unseen hand
Through this dreary desert land.

Canst thou trust the Lord that bought thee,
And with loving kindness sought thee?
I, who called thee by thy name,
I, the Lord, am still the same.

I have seen thy prayers and weeping;
Faithful record I am keeping;
Only to the end endure,
Thou shalt find the promise sure.

I am He who lives forever;
Who from thee my love shall sever?
Not in wrath, my pilgrim child,
I permit this tempest wild.

Thou shalt know, when thus I've proved thee
All the love wherewith I loved thee;
In the fields of heaven shalt see
Light and joy were sown for thee.

Apprehension.

OH! save me from this hour:
In trembling and in fear
My flesh and heart cry out to thee,
For it is drawing near.
Jesus, no eye but thine alone can see
My utter helplessness, my misery

The cross is sharp, O Lord,
And difficult to *bear;*
Yet to refuse it at thy hands,
Thy servant would not dare.
Help me to take it up, and follow thee
Through *shame and pain*, to dark Gethsemane.

There would I look on thee,
  Thou Saviour, in thy woe,
Bleeding in agony for me,
  Bowed meekly down so low;
There would I learn submission to thy will,
Till my rebellious heart is calm and still.

The City of God.

"Heaven lies about us in our infancy."—Wordsworth.

ERE the rose and the roseate hues of the dawn,
  With the dews of my youth, were all scattered and gone;
Ere the cloud, like the far-reaching wing of the night,
Had shut out the glory of God from my sight,
I saw a wide realm in the azure unfold,
Where the fields nodded towards me their flowers of gold;
And the soft airs sailed o'er them, and drop't from above,
As if shed from innumerous pinions of love:

There were trees with broad boles steeped in
perfume and dew,
While their full breasts for ever leaned up to the
blue,
And within their wide bosoms the winds seemed
to rest
With the calm like the sleep of a soul that is blest;
Or, if any light rustle stole out from their limbs,
'Twas the murmurous music of delicate hymns,
As if some dear angel sat singing within
To a spirit just won from the regions of sin:
There were streams which seemed born but in
slumb'rous bowers,
Stealing down, like a dream, through the sleep
of the flowers,—
So pure was the azure they won from the height,
The blue hills seemed melting to rivers of light;
And within their fair realm, where but angels
have trod,
I behold, as I thought, the great City of God!
All its high walls were pierced with no engines
of Death;
No moat, with its dull pool, lay stagnant beneath:
The last bolts, I ween, the stout heart has to fear,
Are pointed and sped from Death's citadel here;
And the last hungry moat the pure soul has to
brave,
Ere it passes the portal to bliss, is the grave!

There the wide wall went East till it dimmed to
the view,
And the wide wall went West till it passed into
blue;
And the broad gates stood open, inviting the way,
Like the hands of the Lord to his children astray.
There were high towers, climbing still dazzlingly
higher,
Till each shone like a fixed guiding pillar of fire;
And the angels who watched on their summits
afar,
So lessened by distance, gleamed each as a star:
And the great dome that templed the Father in
light,
Seemed to swell and to circle, and to swell on the
sight
As some angel, who cleaves his bright way 'mid
the spheres,
Beholds the blue dome of the earth as he nears.
There was music — my soul unto memory yields,
And hears the low sounds floating over the fields;
But, alas! not as then, with its rapturous desire,
Like some bird that sits hushed by the song of a
choir,
It melted and flowed o'er the walls and the towers,
And sweet as if breathed from the lips of the
flowers, —

As if the bright blossoms, with loving accord,
Had risen and sang to the praise of the Lord!
Then I thought 'mid that music to wander and
 wait
For the loved ones, just there by the palm at the
 gate,
To begin the great life that no Death can o'ertake,
And to dream the great dream that no tumult can
 break,
In the broad world of Beauty, of flowers, and
 bliss.
But, alas! I awoke where the thorns grow in this:
And the walls of Death's citadel now intervene,
And the grave, like a moat, yawns here darkly
 between:
But still, through the mists and the shadows of
 night,
I can follow the stars on those pillars of light;
And I know the great gates stand there open and
 broad,
Inviting the way to the CITY OF GOD.

T. B. READ.

Immortality.

BY FRANCIS DE HAES JANVIER.

"O death, where is thy sting? O grave, where is thy victory? Thanks be to God, which giveth us the victory through our Lord Jesus Christ."—1 CORINTHIANS xv. 55, 57.

WHO deems the Saviour dead?
And yet He bowed his head;
And while in sudden night the sun retired,
And, through thick darkness hurled,
Reeled on the shuddering world,
The mighty Son of God, in blood, expired!

Expired, but in the gloom
And silence of the tomb,
Death's mystery unveiled to mortal sight:
Triumphant o'er His foes,
A conqueror He rose,
And from the grave commanded life and light!

And shall we count those dead
For whom the Saviour bled,
And died, and rose, and lives for ever more?
And were the grief, and loss,
The shame, and scourge, and cross,
Endured in vain by Him whom we adore?

And shall His children fear,
When that great hour draws near,
Which gives them immortality with God?
Should not our souls rejoice
To hear our Father's voice,
And gladly take the path the Saviour trod?

Through death's deep shadow lies
Our journey to the skies,
And all beyond is light, and life, and love;
The dead whom we deplore
Have only passed before,
And wait to greet us in the world above!

Then, let the summons come
Which calls our spirits home,
From sin, and pain, and sorrow, ever free;
Where weary ones may rest
Upon that Saviour's breast,
Whose death revealed our immortality!

Christ's Help and All-Sufficiency.

EASY 't were to work my soul's undoing,
Did not Jesus guard life's narrow way.
Day by day my wasted strength renewing,
Helping his own precepts to obey.

Or, the sore temptation he removeth,
When he sees me weak and prone to fall;
In my bare escape his love he proveth,
As, when strong, I triumph over all.

Not to me the glory then remaineth,
When some secret purpose to fulfil;
Still he nerves my arm until it gaineth
Victories surpassing mine own skill.

Nor should it depress, if with his favor
To the lowliest station I am led,
Or while there my weak, sincere endeavor,
Thwarted is, and naught accomplished

All mankind are willing to adore him
While his service yields but this world's gain,
Give me rather grace to walk before him,—
Faithful still, though suffering loss and pain.

Surely such the Saviour hath selected
On their hearts his image to impress;
Shall I murmur — wish myself rejected
From their number whom he most doth bless?

If I robbed were of each earthly treasure,
And my soul meanwhile no increase knew,
Doubting, trembling at such straitened measure,
I might utter lamentations due.

But though outwardly abased, forsaken,
While within his presence I can find,
Looking upward, with a trust unshaken,
Not one want shall move my steadfast mind.

"Me, too!"

"WE'LL seek for flowers in the woods,"
I heard a mother say;
"For in their shady solitudes
My children love to play.
Come, Willie, call the other boys,
Ere falls the evening dew;"
And then another little voice,
Soft pleading, said: "Me, too!"

O childish heart that could not bear
  Her name should be forgot!
O childish love that longed to share
  With all the common lot!
Such tone should ne'er be heard in vain,
  So tremulous and true;
A link in that sweet household chain,
  She claimed her right—"Me, too!"

But not alone in childhood's years
  The heart gives out this cry;
'Tis heard amid the silent tears
  Of life's deep agony.
The lonely soul, athirst for love
  Will cry as infants do;
And lift, all other tones above,
  Its passionate—"Me, too!"

Formed by one hand, we live and die;
  Before one throne we kneel;
The longings of humanity
  Send up one deep appeal.
Our nature's tendrils intertwine,
  Fed by one common dew;
None seek in solitude to pine,
  Each heart throb says: "Me, too!"

God teach us then in rank to stand,
  Firm as brave spirits should;
Joined heart to heart, and hand to hand,
  In holy brotherhood;
And casting off the ice of pride,
  Wear warm hearts mild and true;
Nor from the weakest turn aside,
  Who feebly cries: "Me, too!"

Less and More.

TWO prayers, dear Lord, in one—
  Give me both less and more;
Less of the impatient world, and more of thee;
  Less of myself, and all that heretofore
Made me to slip where willing feet do run,
And held me back from where I fain would be—
    Kept me, my Lord, from thee!

All things which most I need
  Are thine: thou wilt bestow
Both strength and shield, and be my willing guest;
  Yet my weak heart takes up a broken reed,
Thy rod and staff doth readily forego,
And I, who might be rich, am poor, distressed,
    And seek, but have not rest.

How long, O Lord, how long?
  So have I cried of late,
As though I knew not what I well do know:
  Come thou, Great Master-Builder, and create
  Anew that which is thine; undo my wrong—
Breathe on this waste, and life and health bestow:
    Come, Lord, let it be so!

Let it be so, and then—
  What then? My soul shall wait
And ever pray—all prayers, dear Lord, in one—
  Thy will o'er mine in all this mortal state
  Hold regal sway. To thy commands, Amen!
Break from my waiting lips till work is done,
    And crown and glory won!

A. D. F. R.

"Himself hath done it."

"What shall I say? He hath spoken unto me, and himself hath done it."—Isaiah xxxviii. 15.

"HIMSELF hath done it all"—Oh! how those words
  Should hush to silence every murmuring thought!
Himself hath done it—he who loves me best,
  He who my soul with His own blood hath bought.

"Himself hath done it!" Can it then be aught
Than full of wisdom, full of tenderest love?
Not one unneeded sorrow will he send
To teach this wandering heart no more to rove.

"Himself hath done it." Yes, although severe
May seem the stroke, and bitter be the cup,
'Tis his own hand that holds it, and I know
He'll give me grace to drink it meekly up.

"Himself hath done it." Oh! no arm but his
Could e'er sustain beneath earth's dreary lot;
But while I know he's doing all things well,
My heart his loving kindness questions not.

"Himself hath done it!" He who 's searched me through,
Sees how I cleave to earth's ensnaring ties;
And so he breaks each reed on which my soul
Too much for happiness and joy relies.

"Himself hath done it!" He would have me see
What broken cisterns human friends *must* prove,
That I may turn, and quench my burning thirst
At his own fount of *ever*-living love.

"Himself hath done it." Then I fain would say,
Thy will in all things ever more be done,
E'en though that will remove whom best I love:
While Jesus lives *I* cannot be *alone.*

"Himself hath done it,"—precious, precious words,
"Himself," my "Father," "Saviour," "Brother," "Friend,"
Whose faithfulness no variation knows;
Who having loved me, *loves me to the end.*

And when in His eternal presence blest,
I at His feet my crown immortal cast,
I'll gladly own, with all His ransomed saints,
"*Himself hath done it*" all, from *first* to last.

The Impotent Man at the Pool of Bethesda.

St. John v. 2–9.

OH, wondrous faith! that bade the sick man lie,
With heart of hope, and upward-straining eye,
To watch the Angel, with his wing of love,
The sweet, cool waters, unto healing move.
Season by season passed, and still too late,
Another stepped before, and he must wait.

Still did he watch. Sunrise and sunset came,
Summer and winter touched his weary frame,
But, yet, no help for him; still, o'er and o'er,
The "troubled waters" healed another's sore,
And then the pure, bright pool, in sunshine lay;
All power to heal for that time passed away.
The few short words the Holy Spirit told,
As said by him who suffered thus of old,
Are calm and mild; they speak no word of blame
For those who never to his succor came.
Had not the Spirit, through much suffering, wrought
Such meekness, love, and fortitude of thought?
Methinks *He had.* At length, the chastened soul
Hears one inquiring, "Wilt thou be made whole?"
He looks, and sees a human form of love,
Not the bright Angel, o'er the waters move,
And answers simply, as his heart takes heed,
"I have no man" to aid me in my need.
Ah, patient sufferer! *Now* beside thee stands
The Lord of all, who life and death commands;
Who, in all seasons, every day and hour,
Hath healing, mercy, blessing in His power.
Oh, ye who suffer through long, lingering years,
Waiting and watching till your Lord appears,
Be not disheartened! *He* is *near* you still,
Though brain and nerve with doubt and anguish thrill.

Not at *one season* does he come to cure,
But every moment marks what you endure;
Makes a Bethesda of your lonely room,
By day, by night is there to cheer its gloom,
To speak the healing word, or bid the soul,
Even through Death itself, "Be thou made whole!"

Leafless Trees.

LEAFLESS, and stripped, yet are they whole—
They mind me of a Christian soul,
Whose daily strife is almost o'er,
Waiting for entrance at the door.
Greenness and verdure underlies
What seems so poor to mortal eyes,
And what they are, or what have been
Is naught, if so the sap within
The *roots* has grounded strong and firm,
'Gainst autumn blast, or winter storm.

How well defined their outlines lie
Against the back-ground of the sky!
And here again a type we see
Of what a Christian's course should be,

Distinct, and *clear*, that *all* may trace
His shadow and abiding place.
Oh! leafless trees — unto my heart
How sweet the lessons ye impart.
The fragrance of your early Spring,
Your Summer days of blossoming,
The flushing of your Autumn dyes,
Ne'er brought you quite so near the skies
As now, when desolate, ye seem
Against the Heaven itself to lean.
Oh! all our crowns we cast aside,
All ornaments of human pride,
And passing underneath the rod,
Stand naked in the sight of God.
Not blasted, only stripped and bare,
That we may know how *weak we* are.

Oh! leafless trees, your strength renew,
For *all* the sunshine covers you;
Naught now your symmetry can mar,
Ye stand before us as ye are.
Your branches lifted as in prayer,
As tho' ye felt your need of care;
And from His treasury old and new
With garments God will dower you;
For when the keenest storm winds blow,
Your branches shall be wrapt in snow;
And ye shall stand within His sight,
Serenely clad in robes of white;

While even the descending rain
Shall beat upon you not in vain.
For what more beautiful can be
Than wintery frost-work on the tree,
When cold and rain their work have done?
All glorious beneath the sun,
Transparent in the risen light,
Ye *shine* e'en in the Father's sight

Melt snow into the hardened bole,
As melts God's word into the soul.
Yet e'en the quickening germs of life
May sometimes need the pruning-knife,
For by their fruits alone we see
The value of the grafted tree,
"As by their fruits" alone ye know
God's children in this world below.

May seeking souls the lesson take,
And give up *all* for Christ's dear sake;
He asks the blossoms of your Spring,
First tithe of every offering;
Your Summer day in all its prime,
The glory of your Autumn time,—
For ye must stand beneath His eye,
Like leafless trees against the sky.
Disrobed of self, and shorn of pride,
Your sins laid on the *crucified!*

H. L. N.

Sorrowing.

Impromptu, written by a Clergyman in deep affliction, on reading the Hymn, "Be still, my heart, these anxious cares."

MY heart *is* free from anxious care,
'Tis sorrow's shaft that rankles there;
My Lord, do I dishonor Thee
By weeping? Thou hast wept for me!

Hither in safety have I come,
Led by thy hand towards my home;
And still my chequer'd way shall be
The way that Jesus trod for me.

And now, before his mercy-seat,
I all my cares to him commit;
I know his wisdom, power, and love,
Will guide me to my home above.

Refuse to hear the voice of prayer,
Or sympathize in woe or care!
The stars as soon will cease to glow,
Or ocean's tides refuse to flow.

When God shall cease His word to keep,
Or when His watchful eye can sleep,
My heart may *then* forget her faith,
And sink 'neath sorrow — fail in death.

But if His promises are true,
My happy home I'll keep in view;
His arm my staff, His word my stay —
Jesus my life, my truth, my way.

Death of a Believer.

OH! think, that while you're weeping here,
His hand a golden harp is stringing:
And, with a voice serene and clear,
His ransomed soul, without a tear,
His Saviour's praise is singing.

And think that all his pains are fled,
His toils and sorrows closed forever;
While He whose blood for man was shed
Has placed upon his servant's head
A crown that fadeth never.

And think that in that awful day,
  When darkness sun and moon is shading,
The form that 'midst its kindred clay
Your trembling hands prepare to lay,
  Shall rise to life unfading.

Then weep no more for him who's gone
  Where sin and suffering ne'er shall enter;
But on that Great High Priest alone,
Who can for guilt like ours atone,
  Your own affections centre.

And thus, when to the silent tomb
  Your lifeless dust like his is given,
Like faith shall whisper 'mid the gloom,
That yet again, in youthful bloom,
  That dust shall smile in heaven.

DR. HUIE.

To a Friend in Sickness.

SAD, weary days of sickness,
  Beloved friend, are thine;
And o'er thy life the sun of health
  Long since hath ceased to shine;
And oft we bend in sorrow,
  Over thy couch of pain,
And our hopes of brighter days to come
  Are checked, and checked again.

And yet we would not murmur
  At the All-wise decree,
For we know the Saviour's eye of love
  Is watching over thee;
We know thou art His treasure,
  His own peculiar care,
And what He sendeth thee, His grace
  Will give thee strength to bear.

We read in sacred story,
  How once there came a cloud
O'ershadowing the chosen three,
  And their hearts with fear were bowed;

But e'en from out the darkness
  Came there a voice unknown:—
"This, this is my beloved Son:"
  And all their fear was gone.

So when the cloud of sickness
  Enshrouds thee in its gloom,
And thy fainting heart perchance doth dread
    These shadows of the tomb:—
Thou, too, shalt hear a whisper,
  A still small voice, and mild,
"This is thy Saviour and thy Friend,
  Why should'st thou fear, my child?"

Therefore, oh! friend, beloved,
  Let joy with sorrow blend;
The love which chose thee at the first
  Will keep thee to the end.
Soon shall thy days of mourning,
  Thy weary days, be o'er,
And thou within thy Father's house
  Shalt rest for evermore.

And when thy crown thou castest
  Before His glorious throne,
Thou'lt praise Him then for every cross
  Thy pilgrimage hath known.

Praise Him for every sorrow
  That made thy life grow dim,
And taught thee, *less* to trust in earth,
  And *more* to trust in Him.

S. J. W.

Jesus.

THERE is a name I love to hear—
  I love to speak its worth;
It sounds like music in mine ear—
  The sweetest name on earth.

It tells me of a Saviour's love,
  Who died to set me free;
It tells me of his precious blood—
  The sinner's perfect plea.

It tells me of a Father's smile
  Beaming upon His child;
It cheers me through this "little while,"
  Through desert, waste, and wild.

It tells me what a Father hath
  In store for every day,
And though I tread a darksome path,
  Yields sunshine all the way.

It tells of One whose loving heart
  Can feel my deepest woe,
Who in my sorrow bears a part
  That none can bear below.

It bids my trembling soul rejoice;
  It dries each rising tear;
It tells me, in a "still, small voice"—
  To trust, and not to fear.

JESUS! the name I love so well—
  The name I love to hear!
No saint on earth its worth can tell,
  No heart conceive how dear.

This name shall shed its fragrance still
  Along this thorny road—
Shall sweetly smooth the rugged hill
  That leads me up to God.

And there with all the blood-bought throng,
  From sin and sorrow free,
I'll sing the new eternal song
  Of Jesus' love for me.

F. W.

Treasures of Thought.

IF thou hast thrown a glorious thought
  Upon life's common ways,
Should other men the gain have caught,
  Fret not to lose the praise.

Great thinker, often thou shalt find,
  While folly plunders fame,
To thy rich store the crowd is blind,
  Nor knows thy very name.

What matters that, if thou uncoil
  The soul that God has given,
Not in the world's mean eye to toil,
  But in the sight of Heaven?

If thou art true, yet in thee lurks
  For fame a human sigh;
To Nature go, and see how works,
  That handmaid of the sky.

Her own deep bounty she forgets
  Is full of germs and seeds,
Nor glorifies herself, nor sets
  Her flowers above her weeds.

She hides the modest leaves between,
  She loves untrodden roads;
Her richest treasures are not seen
  By any eye but God's.

Accept the lesson. Look not for
  Reward; from out thee chase
All selfish ends, and ask no more
  Than to fulfil thy place.

THE END.

www.ingramcontent.com/pod-product-compliance
Lightning Source LLC
LaVergne TN
LVHW010742120826
845150LV00009B/1399

9781425517458